Salty, Cheesy,
Herby, Crispy
Snackable Bakes

Salty, Cheesy, Herby, Crispy Snackable Bakes

100 Easy-Peasy, Savory Recipes
for 24/7 Deliciousness

Jessie Sheehan

PHOTOGRAPHY BY NICO SCHINCO

Countryman Press

An Imprint of W. W. Norton & Company
Independent Publishers Since 1923

For information about permission to reproduce selections from this book, write to
Permissions, Countryman Press, 500 Fifth Avenue, New York, NY 10110

For information about special discounts for bulk purchases, please contact
W. W. Norton Special Sales at specialsales@wwnorton.com or 800-233-4830

Manufacturing through Imago
Book design by Allison Chi
Production manager: Devon Zahn

Countryman Press
www.countrymanpress.com

An imprint of W. W. Norton & Company, Inc.
500 Fifth Avenue, New York, NY 10110
www.wwnorton.com

978-1-68268-869-4

10 9 8 7 6 5 4 3 2 1

To my dad, a pigs in a blanket
devotee, who passed during
the writing of this book and
who I couldn't have loved more.

Contents

Introduction

Wait, What's a Snackable Bake Again?

Hello, peeps, and welcome to my salty, cheesy, herby, *crispy* snackable bake world. I couldn't be more thrilled to have you. Now, if you, too, are excited to be here, but also just a tiny bit flummoxed as to how exactly one *defines* a "snackable bake," relax. I got you. A snackable bake, in case you missed the memo, is an easy-peasy treat, morsel, snack, item, baked good, delicacy, etc. that can be assembled in minutes, with ingredients already in your pantry and with nothing more than a whisk, a spatula, and a bowl (i.e., snackable bakers rarely fraternize with stand mixers; nor do they vibe all that well with a sinkload of dirty dishes). Moreover, a snackable bake is (typically) enjoyed within an hour or so of its assembly. Long rest times pre-bake, or even postbake, is just not how we roll in snackable bake land.

Snackable Baking × Me

Want to know how I became—I think it's fair to say—*the OG* snackable baker? Oh, good. I'm glad to hear that. Well, I have oft said that I am the "self-proclaimed queen" of easy-peasy (read: "snackable") baking. However, now that I have written not one, but two, books on the topic, I think it might be time to do away with the "self-proclaimed," and just call a queen a queen. I've been easy-peasy baking for a good long while, and although I may have spent a few years way back when "project baking" (aka embracing recipes with loads of fussy ingredients, steps, components, etc.) simple, quick, delicious baked goods are now truly my baking love language. I just can't be bothered with the time and energy (and copious amounts of dirty bowls) more complicated recipes require. Maybe it's my impatient nature? Maybe it's my voracious needs-to-be-satisfied-stat sweet and (now) savory tooth? Maybe it's my hatred of doing dishes? Who can say? All I know is that creating a baked good that calls for only a few basic ingredients—plus, in the case of my savory bakes, a handful of spices—is assembled in a few steps and bakes in less than an hour is my idea of a very good time—and I'm hoping making such a treat is yours, too.

Snackable Baking: the Gift that Keeps on Giving

Now, if you've been paying attention (which I know you have), you might be thinking to yourself, "What? *Salty, cheesy, herby, crispy* snackable bakes? I thought Jessie was into cakes, cookies, and brownies?" (And giant homemade milk chocolate peanut butter cups—if you've *really* been paying attention.) And you're right! I am. But I'm an equal opportunity snackable baker, folks, meaning I can go sweet or I can go savory, and since you're holding this book, I'm thinking you can, too. We snackable bake because easy-peasy is our love language—whether we're talking an effortless single-layer devil's food cake or Jack's Tomato Cobbler with Parmesan Cream Biscuits (page 118).

It's the unfussy speediness of snackable baking that lures *us* in. And the fact that, in this book, we get to snackable bake with ingredients that lean savory—such as cheese and herbs; veggies and meat—well, that's just the ~~cherry~~ salt-n-pepper on top. You see, salty, cheesy, herby, crispy bakes are the (edible) gift that keeps on giving; as they satisfy cravings *all* day long—from Pull-Apart Pimiento Cheese Scones (page 48) in the morning; to Oliver's Spinach and Feta Hand Pies (page 100) in the afternoon to Deep-Dish(ish) Cacio e Pepe Quiche (page 136) at night (with loads of snacks in between).

My sweet tooth knows no bounds, that's facts, but even *I* might not be able to eat cake from sunup 'til sundown. Bottom line, whether you've got boundless teeth like me, or are a cheese-plate-for-dessert kind of peep, I think we can all agree that a savory muffin or scone, cookie, or cracker; or a cheesy veggie-forward bread pudding or strata; or a pizzalike galette topped with pepperoni and ricotta, sounds divine. I mean, a girl's got to eat ALL DAY LONG and if said eats are not only *baked,* but are snackable (aka easy-peasy) to boot, well, then I think it's fair to say we're all 100 percent in, right?

The Easy-Peasy Baking Ethos FTW

In short, it's the snackable bake ethos of making simple, scrumptious bakes with pantry-friendly ingredients in record time that brings all the peeps to the party (or the easy-peasy bakers to the kitchen). And, honestly, when the baking includes cheese, salt, herbs, and spice, the party is pretty spectacular. Thus, within these pages, you'll find straightforward, streamlined recipes for Chive Muffins with Herby Cheese Middles (page 28), a Grilled Cheese Sandwich Tart (i.e., puff pastry and American cheese writ large, page 95), an

Everything Bagel and Cream Cheese Snacking "Bread" (full of cream cheese pockets, briny capers, and loads o' everything spice blend, page 68), a Garlicky Creamed Greens Pie in a melted butter piecrust (page 121), and Dad's Pigs in a Blanket (page 218) made with an easy biscuit dough. They all fit on a single page; have short ingredient lists and easy-to-follow, brief instructions; require no special equipment; and take minutes to prepare. Easy-peasy baking FTW, if you ask me.

Snackable Bakes: A 24/7 Way to Eat

Applying the easy-peasy baking ethos to savory bakes, as I've done herein, is a necessary and fabulous undertaking, if I do say so myself. And one that leaves you the lucky recipient of 100 uncomplicated recipes for all the salty, cheesy, herby, crispy, *utterly* tantalizing things that you can now whip up lickety-split, no matter the time of day. But that's not all. As you've now surmised (you smart little snackable devil, you), snackable bakes of the savory variety are not only crave-worthy, they're also breakfast, lunch, and dinner worthy.

For Breakfast, Lunch, or Dinner

Think: Herby Swiss Dutch Baby (page 139) for brekkie, Smash(ish) Burger Hand Pies with Cheese (page 96) for lunch and for din-din, how about Baked Spaghetti "Pie" with Cheesy Marinara (page 123), served with "Pesto" Snacking "Bread" with Mozzarella (page 71) or Ballymaloe Rosemary Onion "Focaccia" (page 79), if you know what's good for you. No matter the meal, a savory snackable bake is your friend in a pinch, your fallback plan when you're in a rush, and your go-to when foolproof deliciousness is the top priority.

For Your Snacky Pleasure

And in addition to your three squares, salty, cheesy, herby, crispy snackable bakes also make for wonderful small plates—be they of the snacky, appy, or—dare I fancy things up and say—hors d'oeuvres-y variety (girl dinner, anyone?). And what about boards? you might ask. Well, yes: a savory snackable bake board will literally light your board game on fire. I mean, a board adorned with a few small bowls of Roasted Chili Lime Almonds (page 213), Miso Garlic Butter Party Mix (page 209), and Eve's "Cheesy" Buttery Popcorn (page 210), coupled with some Salami, Brie, and Figgy Mini Pies (page 108); Butter Crackers with Melty Cheese and Sour Pickles (page 187); and Cream Cheese and Olive Pinwheels (page 172) is just an example (I'm riffing here) of one of many potential boards that you are def going to want to hang out with. For more fab board inspo, see page 224.

And you know who else is going to want to hang out? Your friends—the ones who invite you over for a drink or dinner. The vast majority of these snacks freeze and travel well. So, don't be afraid to pack them up and head to a pal's. Have board will travel, as they (never) say. And, yes: the younger set, too, are up for a hang with these snacky bakes. I mean, playdate snacks that both grown-ups *and* kids are into? Yup. And if they eat enough, and you throw in some carrot sticks, you might even be able to call it dinner—Best-Ever Cheesy Sausage Balls (page 221) and Baked Mac-n-Cheese Bites (page 201), I'm looking at you.

Some Thoughts on Your Spice Drawer (and Those Fresh Herbs in Your Crisper)

Not sure I am going to be dropping any science here when I tell you that savory snackable bake recipes tend to call for a bunch of different herbs and spices to, well, zhoosh things up. Black pepper, cayenne, red pepper flakes, garlic and onion powders—even mustard powder and paprika—all make appearances in these pages (sometimes over and over again), as do fresh herbs, such as thyme and chives. Now, I didn't include all these flavorful extras to be difficult; in fact, I pulled back as much as I could to avoid a lengthy ingredient list that might result in its reader (aka you) tiptoeing from the kitchen, takeout menu in hand. I used only as much herb and spice as was necessary to make truly delectable, superflavorful, easy-peasy salty, cheesy, herby, crispy bakes. And I hope you find I've succeeded.

The Salty, Cheesy, Herby, Crispy Toolkit and (Very Friendly) Pantry and Fridge

The Toolkit

Yes, you can literally assemble every recipe in this book with a bowl a whisk and a spatula, and I've included my faves here (as well as a few random tools that I have in my kitchen, and that you, if you're interested in twinning with me (which I hope you are), might want to have in yours, too); as well as the pans you'll need for the recipes.

YOUR HANDS: Peeps, it's a cliché for a reason, but your hands are literally your best tool in the kitchen. I use my hands to do everything from separating eggs to mixing dough (or ground meat, as the case may be) to squeezing lemons to sprinkling nuts and seeds. I'm not squeamish or "afraid to get my hands dirty." And you shouldn't be, either. Moreover, particularly in the case of mixing dough or meat, using your hands gives you lots of control, allowing you to ensure everything is properly combined. without overdoing it.

LARGE GLASS BOWL: My forever fave for mixing dough, batter, etc. is a large Pyrex bowl. I particularly love that it is microwave-safe.

WHISK: I love an 11-inch(ish) wire whisk with a comfy silicone handle. GIR makes my favorite one, as I love all the bright colors.

FLEXIBLE SPATULA: I also love GIR's 11-inch silicone spatulas (pink is my favorite spatula color, if you're thinking of gifting me one).

A 2-CUP GLASS LIQUID MEASURING CUP: Pyrex is my fave, but Anchor works, too; as does the plastic OXO one.

BENCH SCRAPER: Oh, gosh: do I ever love my bench scraper. I have one with a wooden handle and one that is all metal; and I use them for everything from cubing butter to scoring and cutting scones to dividing up bread dough when making rolls.

NONSLIP PASTRY MAT: A nonslip pastry mat might seriously be my most coveted tool (and if you knew how much I loved my bench scraper, you'd understand that this is saying a lot). Why, might you ask? Because I detest a mess: if you roll out Magic Melted Butter Pie Dough for hand pies (page 233) or assemble Herby Yogurt Biscuits (page 43) or cut out Pepper Jack Cheese Straws (page 214) on a mat, you avoid having to flour your work surface so generously (if at all). Your dough is just much less likely to stick to the mat than it is to a counter, in the first place. In addition, the mat's dough diame-

ter outlines are a lifesaver when hand-pie making. OXO makes a great silicone version.

MICROWAVE: This feels like the right time to tell you that I adore my microwave (although you may already know this about me). I am very microwave-forward, as I like to say, and I use it all the time when I snackable bake. From melting butter to making 4-Minute Mushrooms (page 238) to steaming spinach for my Spinach Artichoke "Dip" Strata (page 130), my microwave gets a lot of play.

PRECUT PARCHMENT PAPER SHEETS: I won't lie: I'm a precut parchment paper newbie, but the fact that the paper fits perfectly in a standard-size baking sheet and thus removes the need for me to tear it myself, using the (too sharp/not sharp enough) sawtooth metal strip on the box is literally a freaking gift from the baking gods.

WOODEN SKEWERS: I use long wooden skewers to test whether a baked good is ready to be pulled from the oven; toothpicks are too short and the tip of a paring knife too smooth to grab any crumbs (Pro tip: I always remove baked goods from the oven when the tester comes out with a crumb or two, to avoid overbaking.)

KITCHEN SCALE AND OVEN THERMOMETER: I mean, I kinda-sorta feel like *any* baker's toolkit (be they snackable or not) should include a scale (I like the small, brightly colored Escali Primo brand), and an oven thermometer (no preference).

PASTRY BRUSH: It's a good idea to get your hands on a pastry brush when savory snackable baking, as loads o' recipes herein call for The Ultimate Egg Wash (page 230). Salty, cheesy,

herby, crispy snackable bakes often lean matte brown; and an egg wash helps brighten the bakes, providing a glossy, golden finish.

FLEXIBLE BENCH SCRAPER: A great tool for scraping sticky, wet dough from the bowl when no-knead bread making. GIR makes a fab silicone one.

PORTION SCOOPS: I adore a portion scoop (think ice cream scoop) and when muffin, biscuit, and drop scone making, you likely will, too. I have a 1/4-cup scoop and a 1 1/2-tablespoon scoop and I use both of them constantly when snackable baking.

My Pans

MUFFIN TIN: I like a sturdy 12-well standard-size tin (and once you try the Pear, Gorgonzola, and Toasted Walnut Muffins (page 32), get ready to be muffin-ing on a weekly basis).

LOAF PAN: I'm partial to an 8 1/2-by-4 1/2-inch pan, as I prefer the look of a loaf this size to those baked in a 9-by-5-inch pan. My fave pan is the Williams Sonoma Goldtouch Pro.

BAKING SHEET(S): One standard, rimmed, sturdy half-sheet pan (18 by 13 inches) is really all you need, but two is a life changer. I adore the Williams Sonoma Goldtouch Pro Nonstick Non Corrugated pans.

8-INCH SQUARE AND 9-BY-13-INCH RECTANGULAR PANS: When snacking "bread"–baking in my 8-inch or "focaccia"-making in my 9-by-13-inch, the straight sides, sharp corners, nonstick surface, and unprecedented sturdiness of William Sonoma's Goldtouch Pro bakeware gives me all the feels.

8- AND 9-INCH ROUND CAKE PANS: I like sturdy, straight-sided cake pans. 'Nuff said.

MINI MUFFIN TIN: I prefer a mini muffin tin with straight(ish) inner sides, as opposed to sloped wells.

POPOVER PAN: Although Olive Oil Black Pepper Popovers (page 107) *taste* the same when baked in a muffin tin, the lofty stature that the popover pan guarantees is a sight to behold (and sometimes I'm into looks). I like a heavy pan, with tall cups, such as the Nordic Ware Grand Popover Pan.

10- OR 12-INCH CAST-IRON SKILLETS: I'm partial to Lodge brand—they last forever and are affordable. Plus, family heirloom, anyone? If you don't have a 10-inch skillet, for whipping up the Mushroom and Mozzarella Skillet Bread Pudding (page 132), try a 7-by-11-inch or a 9-by-13-inch baking pan. But do so mindfully, as (pro tip) a different pan = a different bake time.

3 1/2-QUART DUTCH OVEN: Although not technically a "pan," and only necessary when baking a few of the no-knead breads, I really do adore my Dutch oven (and, truth be told, I have several—not just a 3 1/2-quart one) and thus highly recommend you make the investment. I'm partial to those made by Le Creuset brand.

The (Very Friendly) Pantry and Fridge Essentials

One of the hallmarks of a snackable bake is that it is chock-full of pantry and fridge-friendly ingredients. Many of those that follow (aka my cheesy, herby, salty, crispy must-haves, as it were) you likely already possess, and if not, a quick trip to the grocery store—or even the corner store/bodega, should set you up ~~sweet~~ savory.

BASIC BAKING INGREDIENTS (I.E. FLOUR, EGGS, KOSHER SALT, LEAVENERS, UNSALTED BUTTER, AND A LITTLE BIT OF SUGAR): I mean, this is a baking book, after all, so you'll need the aforementioned ingredients. Sugar, however, is only ever included in the recipes in fairly tiny amounts; and it's only present for moisture and browning, not sweetness.

CHEESE: I can't tell you how close I came to dedicating this book to cheese. Okay, not really, but I mean, I love it, you likely love it, and it plays a starring role in so many of the recipes herein. But don't worry if your cheese drawer isn't always stocked with the fanciest varieties—remember, this is an easy-peasy baking book, thus all the cheeses called for in the recipes are easily found in your local grocery store. Also, it's worth mentioning that much of it is shredded, and although this is likely a controversial position, I totally support you if you want to buy the preshredded stuff. I am a big fan of shortcuts, and the convenience that is a bag of pre-prepped cheese, is one of my all-time fave cuts.

CREAM CHEESE: What can I say? Cream cheese is my everything and finds its way into a couple of different recipes herein.

MAYONNAISE: Okay, so here's the thing: I really do love mayo (Hellman's brand specifically), and thus always (like *always*) have it in my fridge. But you will see mayo in so many of these recipes, not because I am such a fan and not in the way you'd expect. I brush many of my hand pies with mayo before filling them; I brush the biscuit dough that blankets my dogs with it before wrapping said dogs; I brush the puff pastry that makes up the "bread" of my grilled cheese tart with it; and more. And I do this because mayo adds a wonderful richness and subtle unidentifiable flavor to all of these items that you can't quite put your finger on. It has a mysterious unctuousness that just makes everything tastier.

DRIED HERBS AND SPICES: Onion and garlic powders make many appearances throughout this book, to bring those *flavors* to the recipes, without the attendant mincing (though a shortcut exists when it comes to garlic; see next item), chopping, sautéing, and browning of it all. Dried oregano, thyme, red pepper flakes, cayenne pepper, mustard powder, and paprika also show up now and again.

JARRED MINCED GARLIC: What can I say? I always have a jar of minced garlic in the fridge because the act of mincing fresh garlic is one of my least favorites (and is only ever even tolerable with a garlic press—sorry, haters). I once read that Julia Turshen encourages cooking shortcuts, such as jarred garlic, as long as said shortcut motivates one to cook more. And I think she was basically talking to me. If jarred garlic will move you to make Why, Bonjour! A Loaf (page 60)—a Parmesan, garlic, and herb tea bread that I wish I was eating right now—then just know that Julia and I are both *very* happy.

NONSTICK COOKING SPRAY: Yes, using cooking spray is a tiny bit contentious, but it also happens to have a permanent (coveted) place in my

pantry (see pages 21–23 for the why of it all). I prefer Pam brand.

SALTED BUTTER (FOR SERVING): Although I use *un*salted butter as an ingredient in my baking, for serving, I reach for salted.

The Friendly(ish) Pantry and Fridge Essentials

FRESH HERBS: Oh, herbs, how I love/hate you. I mean, I *love* how the Mini Irish Soda Bread Scones with Cheddar and Thyme (page 55) really do sing when there's fresh thyme in the mix. And I *adore* how the Mushroom Cap Pasties (page 103) literally come to life when you add a little parsley. I mean, honestly, I wouldn't want you to sub dried in either recipe. Fresh herbs provide flavor and even texture that you can't replicate with the dried stuff (as much as I wish it was otherwise). But do I like prepping and chopping herbs? Um . . . no. I get agita when removing tiny tender leaves from woody stems and my subpar knife skills also don't do me any favors in the herb department. And if you feel similarly, I get you. But I'm hoping that, despite your reservations, you're like me, and bottom line, we're here for the freshies, and the brightness that they add to our bakes.

BACON, PROSCIUTTO (THICKLY AS WELL AS THINLY SLICED), CHORIZO, SAUSAGE, HAM, GROUND BEEF, SALAMI, ETC.: Yes, peeps: there is meat in this book. But, good news: if meat is not your thing, you can (almost) ALWAYS leave it out.

STORE-BOUGHT PUFF PASTRY: I adore store-bought puff pastry and am hoping that, after diving into the "Toasty Handhelds" chapter,

where it features heavily, and whipping up the Baby Ham and Cheese "Croissants" (page 91) and Pom's Boxing Day Sausage Rolls (page 92), among other utterly yummy treats, you will, too. Pepperidge Farm brand makes a great puff and it is easy to find.

FLAKY SEA SALT: A sprinkle of flaky sea salt (I'm fond of Maldon) is the chef's finishing (good-bye?) kiss to so many of these recipes. I love its crunchy texture and the way it pops the flavors of the baked goods it smooches.

SEEDS: I mean, who knew that little old marshmallow-loving me would write a book that required its readers to buy seeds, but that's what happens when you write a recipe for Seedy Sesame Crackers with Oats (page 183) and another for your seed-obsessed husband, aptly titled "Matty's" Nutty Seed Brown Bread (page 67). Since seed-loving peeps seem to be everywhere, you shouldn't have any trouble tracking down the ones called for here.

CAKE FLOUR: A variety of recipes are based on—or actually call for—my Best-Ever Cream Biscuit Dough (page 234), and they all require cake flour, in addition to all-purpose, as I believe the tenderness it imparts is worth the fact that it's an extra, slightly finicky ingredient. But I get it that cake flour may not be on very close terms with your pantry. Thus, to avoid forcing you to make the dreaded "special trip" to the grocery store, I'm going to teach you **to make cake flour:** place 1 cup (130 g) of all-purpose flour in a bowl, remove 2 tablespoons of it and replace with 2 tablespoons of cornstarch, whisk, and voilà: cake flour. Cake flour is finer than all-purpose and the substitution of the cornstarch, for some of the all-purpose, results in a flour more similar in texture to cake flour, than to all-purpose.

WHOLE WHEAT FLOUR: I never used to make room for whole wheat flour in my pantry (call me narrow-minded) but the Whole Wheat Buttermilk Soda Bread with Pecans (page 76), "Matty's" Nutty Seed Brown Bread (page 67), and Seeded Olive Oil Whole Wheat Boule (page 157) all call for it, and since developing these three recipes, there's been some mind expansion happening, I'm pleased to report.

ZA'ATAR: Za'atar is a deliciously fragrant and flavorful Middle Eastern spice blend that often includes oregano, plus sesame seeds, sumac, and salt; and is just wonderful (due to its kind of pizza-y vibe) with my Tomato Za'atar Galette with Onion and Cheese (page 124) and in my Za'atar, Feta Cheese, and Lemon Snacking "Bread" (page 69). See page 58 for a recipe for homemade za'atar.

JARRED MARINARA SAUCE: You'll need it for my Baked Spaghetti "Pie" with Cheesy—you guessed it—Marinara (page 123), the Pepperoni "Pizza" Galette with Ricotta (page 126), and the Marinara Pizza (a variation of the Anchovy Onion one, page 162). Because I am a big fan of a jarred sauce, I always have it in the pantry for pasta with red sauce–craving emergencies. But if you'd rather make sauce from scratch, Marcella Hazan has an easy recipe, calling for nothing but canned tomatoes, butter, and onions, which I adore.

NUTRITIONAL YEAST: I'm in a fairly new relationship with cheesy, umami-rich nutritional yeast, and I'm completely smitten. FYI, it is a game

changer when sprinkled over Eve's "Cheesy" Buttery Popcorn (page 210), or "Pizza Crackers" (see Fire Crackers variation, page 184).

CHILI CRISP: I'm obsessed with Fly by Jing brand chili crisp, and just chili crisp in general, and thus find myself drizzling it over everything, including my Chili Crisp Sour Cream Flatbreads with Melty Cheese (page 104) and Dolly's Melty Cheese Squares with Chili Crisp (page 222). Oh, and I've got a tip on page 104 for creating a bit more chili-infused oil when your jar runs low.

HOT PEPPER JELLY: Wowza, do I ever love hot pepper jelly, and the combo of it and cream cheese in my Hot Pepper Jelly and Cream Cheese–Stuffed Muffins (page 31) is just too good to be true. Buy a jar, thank me later.

Final Salty, Cheesy, Herby, Crispy Thoughts and a Tip

- **"You Do You"** is kind of a big theme in this book as, in my opinion, savory baking lends itself more to riffing than sweet baking does. But I won't lie; I'm kinda-sorta extremely ambivalent about giving you so much freedom, as I am a control freak in recovery. And so, if you want to switch up the cheese or herb or spice in any and every recipe herein, you have my (reluctant) blessing. But if you're a little afraid of me (JK!) to brazenly go out on your own, guess what? Many of the recipes have exciting variations that will give you all the thrills of a cook who riffs, without the anxiety.

- Snackable baking typically requires a greased pan and in this book, that **grease is**

always cooking spray. I've been hooked on the efficiency and efficacy of cooking spray since working in a professional bakery, almost 20 years ago. It isn't messy to apply, like softened butter can be, and it is the speediest pan-greasing technique I know. Yet, cooking spray makes some people extremely upset and I get that. Thus, if spray is not your cup of tea, and you are a grease-with-softened-butter kind of person, by all means use it.

- When I bake, I always **rotate the pan** halfway through the baking period. And if there is more than one item of deliciousness in the oven, I always swap the position of said items after I rotate. I picked up this tip when working with commercial ovens, which can be a bit wonky, and I still do it today due to *my own* oven's hot spots. The right side always bakes slower than the left (so if you're coming over to bake me something, consider yourself warned). But here's the thing: if your oven has never given you a lick of trouble, then, first of all, please share the make and model as I am purchasing one now; and second, you can ignore the rotating instruction. A lot of bakers never do it and turn out fab baked goods every time.

- Some of the baked goods herein really benefit from a short stint in the freezer prebake, particularly the savory cookies and a couple of the snacks. And in case you are worried about the size of your freezer and the impossibility of fitting, for instance, a sheet pan of Kristin's Olive and Cheese Puffs (page 207) into it, no worries: if I ask you to **freeze an item on a baking sheet**, you can use a dinner plate (or two) instead.

- Stop the presses: I now **weigh liquid ingredients!** This is a huge shift for me, as I have always measured liquid by volume in a spouted glass measuring cup and have used milliliters just to seem like a team player. But I am done with all that and now use gram measurements for everything from water to milk to oil (you'll still see cup measurements, for those that are volume-inclined. Me, though? I'm grams or go home).

- So, I have this tip for **melting and slightly cooling butter** simultaneously that always bears repeating. Several recipes in this book call for melted butter (as snackable bakers avoid creaming softened butter at all costs, due to our disdain for stand mixers), and when you come upon one, I want you to do this: melt the butter ONLY until there are still a few small chunks of solid butter floating around (and if we're twinning, you'll be doing the melting in a covered, microwave-safe bowl in the microwave). And then, off the heat, whisk in the chunks. As you whisk the solid butter into the melted, the whisking in and of itself, plus the ensuing melting of the little chunks, will help to bring down the temperature of the butter. Recipes rarely call for superhot melted butter, and this technique results in melted yet cooled butter; which is kind of the (buttery) gold standard.

CHAPTER 1

Savory Muffins and Biscuits and Scones— Oh My!

This would NOT be an easy-peasy savory baking book if it did not include a chapter of salty, cheesy, herby, crispy muffins, biscuits, and scones, am I right? In my opinion, they are the perfect gateway recipes when embarking on your simple (but not sweet) baking journey: they're easy to assemble, quick as a wink to bake (the muffins, for instance, *literally* take 15 minutes), and they're familiar, yet not . . . I mean, you might have stuffed a muffin with cream cheese before, but have you ever stuffed one with hot pepper jelly *and* cream cheese? And maybe you've eaten a date scone, but one with Manchego and chorizo as well? I think not. Finally, is a butter-swim biscuit even part of your vocabulary? If so, wow: I love you even more than I thought I did. And if not, hold on to you easy-peasy baking hat, cause are you ever in for a treat.

Pro Tips, Fun Facts, and Storing/Reheating Instructions

- Muffins, biscuits, and scones bake quickly, so if it seems silly to you to **rotate the pan** during such a brief bake, skip it.

- Muffins, biscuits, and scones **LOVE a good egg wash** and it def provides them with the best color. But if that reads fussy to you, and the recipe calls for melted butter or cream, either makes for a fine substitute.

- Leave your biscuit cutters in the drawer (rolling and cutting and then rerolling scraps is not the easy-peasy baker's idea of a very good time). We **scoop biscuits** in snackable bake land.

- These **biscuit recipes require cake flour** for the most tender of textures. But you can make your own (see page 20)!

- If you're thinking of sleeping on the sweet potato biscuits, because you're feeling lazy about having to bake them, first, I feel you and you are my snackable soulmate, and second, I got you: there's an **easy microwave hack (page 40) for "baking" a sweet potato, stat**.

TO STORE: Muffins, biscuits, and scones are best eaten the day they are made, fresh from the oven and still warm, but will last up to 3 days, tightly wrapped, overnight in the refrigerator if they have cheese, and on the counter if they do not; or in the freezer for up to a month.

TO REHEAT: Reheat room-temperature muffins, biscuits, and scones in a 300°F oven on a parchment-lined baking sheet until warm, about 10 minutes.

Chive Muffins

WITH HERBY CHEESE MIDDLES

MAKES 12 MUFFINS
ACTIVE TIME: 15 MINUTES
BAKE TIME: 15 TO 18 MINUTES

About 5 ounces (150 g) soft,
  herby cheese, such as
  Boursin, cold
½ cup (100 g) vegetable oil
3 tablespoons packed light
  brown sugar
2 large eggs
1 cup (230 g) full-fat sour cream
1 tablespoon baking powder
½ teaspoon baking soda
1 teaspoon kosher salt
½ teaspoon freshly ground
  black pepper
2 cups (260 g) all-purpose flour
¼ cup (11 g) minced fresh
  chives, plus more
  for sprinkling
The Ultimate Egg Wash
  (page 230)
Flaky sea salt for sprinkling

Boursin cheese has been a fave of mine since childhood and stuffing it into a chive muffin is nothing short of genius (thank you very much). The soft cheesy middles and sprinkle of flaky sea salt postbake are the perfect accompaniment to the muffins' bouncy, chive-studded crumb. There's a little sugar in these, to help with browning and moisture, and the egg wash ensures they look as good as they taste. Yes, an egg wash is a tiny bit of extra work, but it provides your baked goods with such gorgeous color *and* you can keep it tightly wrapped in the refrigerator for up to a week.

1. Heat the oven to 400°F. Generously grease a 12-well muffin tin with cooking spray.

2. Divide the cheese into 12 scant 1-tablespoon portions. Flatten them into disks about 1½ inches in diameter, place them on a parchment-lined plate, and chill them in the refrigerator while you make the batter. Whisk together the oil and brown sugar in a large bowl. Whisk in the eggs, one at a time, and then the sour cream. Vigorously whisk in the baking powder, then the baking soda, and then the salt and pepper. Gently fold in the flour and chives with a flexible spatula—the batter will be thick.

3. Fill each prepared muffin well with about 1½ tablespoons of batter, gently press a chilled cheese disk into each one, and evenly cover with the remaining batter. With damp fingers or a small offset spatula, smooth the tops and brush with egg wash. Sprinkle with a little flaky salt and a few extra chives.

4. Bake for 15 to 18 minutes, until a wooden skewer inserted into the side of a muffin comes out with a moist crumb or two (try to avoid sticking it into the cheesy middle). Remove from the oven and let cool for about 5 minutes, or until you can safely touch the pan without burning yourself. Gently pull the warm muffins from the tin, running a small offset spatula or butter knife around the edges if they resist, and place on a serving plate. Serve warm for middles that are melty and extra soft.

Hot Pepper Jelly and Cream Cheese–Stuffed Muffins

MAKES 12 MUFFINS
ACTIVE TIME: 15 MINUTES
BAKE TIME: 15 TO 18 MINUTES

½ cup (113 g) unsalted butter, melted and cooled slightly

3 tablespoons granulated sugar

2 large eggs

1 cup (227 g) buttermilk

1 tablespoon baking powder

½ teaspoon baking soda

1 teaspoon kosher salt

½ teaspoon freshly ground black pepper

2 teaspoons red pepper flakes

2 cups (260 g) all-purpose flour

6 ounces (170 g) full-fat cream cheese, at room temperature

⅓ cup (105 g) hot pepper jelly, plus more for brushing

The Ultimate Egg Wash (page 230)

I know playing favorites as a mom is frowned upon, but wow—do I ever love these muffin babies o'mine. Something about the heat and vinegar of the jelly combined with the creamy mild, slightly tangy cream cheese is just spectacular here. If you can't find hot pepper jelly, any savory jelly will work, such as red pepper, onion, or bacon. Or make your own: whisk together ¾ cup of apricot or peach jam, 1 teaspoon of cayenne pepper, or to taste, a rounded ¼ teaspoon of kosher salt, and 2 teaspoons of vinegar.

1. Heat the oven to 400°F. Generously grease a 12-well muffin tin with cooking spray.

2. Whisk together the butter and sugar in a large bowl. Whisk in the eggs, one at a time, and then the buttermilk. Vigorously whisk in the baking powder, then the baking soda, and then the salt, black pepper, and red pepper flakes. Gently fold in the flour with a flexible spatula—the batter will be thick.

3. Fill each prepared muffin well with about 1½ tablespoons of batter and use a small offset spatula to spread the batter over the bottom of the well. Divide the cream cheese into twelve 1-tablespoon (14 g) portions and drop one into each batter-filled well. Spoon a scant 2 teaspoons of jelly on top of the cream cheese, and evenly cover with the remaining batter, a generous 1½ tablespoons per well. With damp fingers or a small offset spatula, spread the batter to the edges of the wells and brush with egg wash.

4. Bake for 15 to 18 minutes, until a wooden skewer inserted in the side of a muffin comes out with a moist crumb or two (try to avoid sticking it into the cheesy middle). Remove from the oven and let cool for about 5 minutes, or until you can safely touch the pan without burning yourself. Place a spoonful or two of jelly in a small bowl and stir to loosen. Brush the muffin tops with the loosened jelly. Gently pull the warm muffins from the tin, running a small offset spatula or butter knife around the edges if they resist, and place on a serving plate. Serve immediately, with extra jelly and cream cheese.

Pear, Gorgonzola, and Toasted Walnut Muffins

These cuties are essentially a cheese plate in a muffin, and the sweet chunks of pear and toasty walnuts temper the funky (and delicious) soft and oozy Gorgonzola pockets. The pears don't need peeling and I've been known to buy pre-crumbled cheese (sorry haters).

MAKES 12 MUFFINS
ACTIVE TIME: 15 MINUTES
BAKE TIME: 17 TO 20 MINUTES

½ cup (100 g) olive oil

3 tablespoons granulated sugar

2 large eggs

1 cup (240 g) full-fat yogurt (not Greek)

1 tablespoon baking powder

½ teaspoon baking soda

1 teaspoon kosher salt

½ teaspoon freshly ground black pepper

2 cups (260 g) all-purpose flour

1 cup (140 g) cored and finely diced pears, no need to peel

1 cup (100 g) walnuts, toasted and finely chopped

2 cups (260 g) Gorgonzola, crumbled

The Ultimate Egg Wash (page 230)

1. Heat the oven to 400°F. Generously grease a 12-well muffin tin with cooking spray.

2. Whisk together the oil and sugar in a large bowl. Whisk in the eggs, one at a time, and then the yogurt. Vigorously whisk in the baking powder, then the baking soda, and then the salt and pepper. Gently fold in the flour, pears, walnuts, and cheese with a flexible spatula.

3. Evenly divide the batter among the 12 prepared wells, about a rounded ¼ cup for each, using a portion scoop, if you have one, or a measuring cup. Brush the tops with egg wash.

4. Bake for 17 to 20 minutes, until a wooden skewer inserted in the center comes out with a moist crumb or two. Remove from the oven and let cool for about 5 minutes, or until you can safely touch the pan without burning yourself. Gently pull the warm muffins from the tin, running a small offset spatula or butter knife around the edges if they resist, and place on a serving plate. Serve immediately.

VARIATION

For Devils on Horseback Muffins, substitute 1 cup packed (145 g) coarsely chopped Medjool dates (about ¾ inch pieces) for the pears, and ⅓ cup packed (50 g) diced cooked bacon (100 g of uncooked bacon—see page 241 for Fast and Dirty (Not Literally) Bacon for the walnuts.

Jalapeño Corn Muffins

MAKES 12 MUFFINS
ACTIVE TIME: 10 MINUTES
BAKE TIME: 14 TO 18 MINUTES

6 tablespoons (85 g) unsalted butter, melted and cooled slightly

¼ cup (50 g) vegetable oil

3 tablespoons packed light brown sugar

2 large eggs

1 cup (230 g) full-fat sour cream

2 teaspoons baking powder

½ teaspoon baking soda

1 teaspoon kosher salt

½ teaspoon freshly ground black pepper

1 cup (130 g) all-purpose flour

1 cup (145 g) medium-grind cornmeal

¼ cup plus 2 tablespoons (67 g) coarsely chopped pickled sliced jalapeños, plus 12 whole slices for decorating

The Ultimate Egg Wash (page 230)

Softened salted butter for serving

I really wanted to include the words "sour cream" in the title of these muffins, as it plays such an important role in their moist texture and slightly tangy flavor, which then works so terrifically with the subtle chew from the corn and the vinegar-forward flavor of the jarred jalapeños. Moreover, the combo of the finely chopped jalapeños, plus the decorative slice on top, means that these muffs are not only pretty, but each has more than a little kick, to boot (pun intended).

1. Heat the oven to 400°F. Generously grease a 12-well muffin tin with cooking spray.

2. Whisk together the melted butter, oil, and brown sugar in a large bowl. Whisk in the eggs, one at a time, and then the sour cream. Vigorously whisk in the baking powder, then the baking soda, and then the salt and pepper. Gently fold in the flour, cornmeal, and jalapeños with a flexible spatula.

3. Evenly divide the batter among the 12 prepared wells, about ¼ cup for each, using a portion scoop, if you have one, or a measuring cup. Brush the tops with egg wash, and place a single slice of jalapeño on top of each.

4. Bake for 14 to 18 minutes, until a wooden skewer inserted in the center comes out with a moist crumb or two. Remove from the oven and let cool for about 5 minutes, or until you can safely touch the pan without burning yourself. Gently pull the warm muffins from the tin, running a small offset spatula or butter knife around the edges if they resist, and place on a serving plate. Serve immediately, with softened salted butter.

Apple Cheddar Muffins

MAKES 12 MUFFINS

ACTIVE TIME: 10 TO 15 MINUTES

BAKE TIME: 15 TO 20 MINUTES

½ cup (113 g) unsalted butter, melted and cooled slightly

3 tablespoons granulated sugar

2 large eggs

1 cup (240 g) whole milk

1 tablespoon plus 1 teaspoon baking powder

1 teaspoon kosher salt

½ teaspoon freshly ground black pepper

½ teaspoon cayenne pepper, or to taste

2 cups (260 g) all-purpose flour

2 cups (200 g) shredded extra-sharp Cheddar, plus more for sprinkling

1 cup (115 g) peeled, cored, and diced apple (about 1 large apple), such as Granny Smith

The Ultimate Egg Wash (page 230)

Softened salted butter for serving (optional)

The combination of apples and Cheddar makes me think of an apple pie with a Cheddar crust—and I'm all in for a savory muffin that gives me sweet-pie vibes. The softened, tangy, just slightly sweet cubes of apple are the perfect match for the melty sharp Cheddar pockets. And melty cheese FTW anywhere and everywhere but *particularly* in a fruit-stuffed muffin. (Lightly) sweet and savory for the win.

1. Heat the oven to 400°F. Generously grease a 12-well muffin tin with cooking spray.

2. Whisk together the melted butter and sugar in a large bowl. Whisk in the eggs, one at a time, and then the milk. Vigorously whisk in the baking powder, and then the salt, black pepper, and cayenne. Gently fold in the flour, cheese, and apples with a flexible spatula.

3. Evenly divide the batter among the prepared 12 wells, about a rounded ¼ cup for each, using a portion scoop, if you have one, or a measuring cup. Brush the tops with egg wash and sprinkle with a little extra shredded Cheddar.

4. Bake for 15 to 20 minutes, until a wooden skewer inserted in the center comes out with a moist crumb or two. Remove from the oven and let cool for about 5 minutes, or until you can safely touch the pan without burning yourself. Gently pull the warm muffins from the tin, running a small offset spatula or butter knife around the edges if they resist, and place on a serving plate. Serve immediately, with or without softened salted butter (these cuties are pretty cheesy and really don't need it—and you can trust me since I am extremely butter-forward).

Salt-n-Pep Skillet Biscuits

MAKES 10 BISCUITS
ACTIVE TIME: 10 MINUTES
BAKE TIME: ABOUT 20 MINUTES

1 cup (130 g) all-purpose flour
1 cup (120 g) cake flour
1½ tablespoons granulated
   sugar
1 tablespoon plus 1 teaspoon
   baking powder
1½ teaspoons kosher salt
1 teaspoon freshly ground
   black pepper, plus more
   for sprinkling
1½ cups (360 g) heavy cream
The Ultimate Egg Wash
   (page 230)
Flaky sea salt for sprinkling
Softened salted butter
   for serving

These are the simplest yet most tender and flavorful biscuits I know; and the fact that they are pull-apart makes me love them all the more (the sides of a pull-apart biscuit are just the softest of all and the most deserving of a thick slathering of softened salted butter). Yes, cake flour does indeed contribute to their otherworldly texture, and it is a somewhat fussy ingredient, and not one necessarily found in the savory snackable baker's pantry. But there's a great hack for turning all-purpose flour into cake flour (see page 20), or, you can just sub additional all-purpose. I love the color that the egg wash brings, but brushing with additional heavy cream works, too.

1. Heat the oven to 425°F. Grease a 10-inch cast-iron skillet with cooking spray.

2. Whisk together the flours, sugar, baking powder, salt, and pepper in a large bowl. Pour the cream over the flour mixture and stir with a flexible spatula just until no loose flour remains.

3. Scoop the dough into 10 biscuits, using a ¼-cup portion scoop, if you have one, or a measuring cup, and evenly space them in the skillet. Brush each biscuit with the egg wash and sprinkle with flaky salt and more pepper.

4. Bake for about 20 minutes, or until the tops and bottoms of the biscuits are nicely browned. Remove from the oven and let them cool in the skillet for about 5 minutes before serving with loads of softened salted butter.

Sweet Potato Cream Biscuits

MAKES 10 BISCUITS
ACTIVE TIME: 10 MINUTES
BAKE TIME: 15 TO 20 MINUTES

1 cup (130 g) all-purpose flour
1 cup (120 g) cake flour
1 tablespoon plus 1 teaspoon
    baking powder
1 teaspoon kosher salt
½ teaspoon freshly grated
    nutmeg
1½ tablespoons packed light
    brown sugar
1 cup (240 g) heavy cream
1 cup (220 g) fresh mashed
    sweet potato, chunky(ish),
    not smooth
The Ultimate Egg Wash
    (page 230)
Softened salted butter
    for serving

With the most spectacular of hues, the sweet potatoes in these biscuits also provide a little "earthy sweetness," to quote my beloved recipe tester Steph. But truly, they are here for little more than the color and tenderness they impart. As such, these biscuits are the perfect blank (orange!) canvas for your fave herbs, spices—even cheese! Canned sweet potatoes will work here, but it's supereasy and fast to whip up a baked one in the microwave (stab it all over with a fork, wrap it in wet paper towel, and microwave it on HIGH for 7 to 10 minutes, rotating it periodically and re-dampening the towel, if necessary, until soft). These biscuits are utterly delicious with a slice of salty ham and a smear of mustard.

1. Heat the oven to 425°F. Line a baking sheet with parchment paper.

2. Whisk together the flours, baking powder, salt, and nutmeg in a large bowl. Whisk together the brown sugar, cream, and mashed sweet potato until almost smooth, but still a little chunky, in a 4-cup measuring cup, if you have one, or medium bowl. Pour the sweet potato mixture over the flour mixture and stir with a flexible spatula just until no loose flour remains—the batter will be thick.

3. Scoop the dough into 10 biscuits, using a ¼-cup portion scoop, if you have one, or a measuring cup, and evenly space them on the prepared sheet. Brush each biscuit with the egg wash.

4. Bake for 15 to 20 minutes, until the tops and bottoms of the biscuits are nicely browned. Remove from the oven and let the biscuits cool on the baking sheet for about 5 minutes before placing on a serving plate. Enjoy with softened butter of the salted variety.

Herby Yogurt Biscuits

MAKES 9 BISCUITS
ACTIVE TIME: 10 MINUTES
BAKE TIME: 17 TO 20 MINUTES

2 cups (260 g) all-purpose flour, plus more for sprinkling

1 cup (120 g) cake flour

1½ tablespoons granulated sugar

1 tablespoon baking powder

½ teaspoon baking soda

1 teaspoon kosher salt

¼ cup (15 g) finely chopped mixed fresh herbs, such as chives and dill, plus 9 dill sprigs, or your fave, for decorating the top of each biscuit

1 cup (240 g) full-fat yogurt (not Greek)

½ cup (113 g) unsalted butter, melted and cooled slightly

The Ultimate Egg Wash (page 230)

Softened salted butter for serving

After wistfully dreaming about a world in which one could make biscuits from melted butter, my bestie, the internet, confirmed that melted butter biscuits is, in fact, a thing. And being a melted butter baker from way back, I went to work. The yogurt here adds wonderful tang and tenderness (thanks, Serious Eats, for the inspo), resulting in a biscuit that splits easily. A combo of woody and soft herbs works best here.

1. Heat the oven to 425°F. Line a baking sheet with parchment paper.

2. Whisk together the flours, sugar, baking powder, baking soda, salt, and chopped herbs in a large bowl. Whisk together the yogurt and melted butter in a 4-cup measuring cup, if you have one, or a medium bowl (don't worry if the butter solidifies a little while you do this). Pour the yogurt mixture into the flour mixture and stir with a flexible spatula until no loose flour remains.

3. Turn out the dough onto a lightly floured work surface and sprinkle just a bit of flour on top. Pat out the dough into a 6-inch square, about 1½ inches tall. Using a bench scraper or a chef's knife, cut the dough into nine square biscuits and evenly space them on the prepared baking sheet. Brush each biscuit with the egg wash and decorate its top with a dill sprig.

4. Bake for 17 to 20 minutes, until the tops and bottoms of the biscuits are nicely browned. Remove from the oven and let cool on the baking sheet for about 5 minutes before placing them on a serving plate. Enjoy with loads of softened salted butter.

Cheesy Butter-Swim Old Bay Biscuits

MAKES 9 BISCUITS

ACTIVE TIME: 10 MINUTES

BAKE TIME: ABOUT 20 MINUTES

10 tablespoons (141 g) unsalted butter

1½ cups (195 g) all-purpose flour

1 cup (120 g) cake flour

1½ tablespoons granulated sugar

1 tablespoon plus 1½ teaspoons baking powder

1 teaspoon kosher salt

2 teaspoons garlic powder

2 teaspoons Old Bay Seasoning, plus ¼ teaspoon more for sprinkling

1 teaspoon onion powder

2 cups (200 g) shredded extra-sharp Cheddar

1½ cups (360 g) whole milk

Allow me to introduce you to my new favorite biscuit—I mean, of course, I love all my biscuit babies and want you to, too, but these salty, cheesy butter-swims are pretty special, with their craggy tops, tall stature, and unique assembly (melted butter is poured into a baking pan, topped with biscuit dough and baked—so cool, right?). Not only do they take the prize for best name, but the combo of Cheddar and Old Bay is the stuff of legends (Red Lobster legends, to be exact). Old Bay Seasoning is a blend of 18 spices, including black and red pepper, paprika, and celery salt. It's packaged in the most fab little yellow can with a red lid and is worth getting your hands on, stat, for butter-swim biscuit making and more.

1. Heat the oven to 450°F. Place the butter in an 8-inch square baking pan and melt it in the oven while it heats—but don't forget about it; you want it just melted, not browned and sputtering.

2. Whisk together the flours, sugar, baking powder, salt, garlic powder, Old Bay, onion powder, and cheese in a large bowl. Pour the milk into the flour mixture and fold with a flexible spatula until combined—the dough will be wet and a little loose. Scrape the biscuit dough into the melted butter–filled pan and pat it evenly over the butter, using a spatula or your hands—the butter will seep up and around the edges of the dough; don't be alarmed. Roughly cut the dough into nine equal-size biscuits with a bench scraper or butter knife.

3. Bake for about 20 minutes, or until the tops of the biscuits are nicely browned. Remove from the oven and sprinkle the biscuits with the extra ¼ teaspoon of Old Bay. Let them cool in the pan for about 5 minutes before serving—these cuties swim in butter, so they actually don't need to be spread with it (but if you're feeling "extra," like we were the day we photographed these, then by all means go for it).

Sage Butter Scones

Melting the butter for these rich, slightly crumbly scones—rather than cutting it in cold—not only shortens the assembly process (you're welcome), but if you melt the butter along with the minced sage, it also helps pop the sage's wonderfully woodsy, earthy and peppery flavor. Yes, I do this in a microwave in a 2-cup glass liquid measuring cup, but the stovetop works, too. Sage, it's not just for stuffing anymore . . .

MAKES 8 SCONES
ACTIVE TIME: 10 MINUTES
BAKE TIME: 17 TO 20 MINUTES

½ cup (113 g) unsalted butter
2 tablespoons minced fresh sage, plus 8 whole leaves for decorating
2 cups (260 g) all-purpose flour
1½ tablespoons granulated sugar
1 tablespoon baking powder
1 teaspoon kosher salt
½ cup (120 g) heavy cream
The Ultimate Egg Wash (page 230)
Softened salted butter for serving

1. Heat the oven to 400°F. Line a baking sheet with parchment paper.

2. Melt the butter, along with the minced sage, either in a 2-cup glass measuring cup or a glass bowl in a microwave on HIGH, or in a small saucepan on the stovetop. Set aside to infuse while you assemble the remaining ingredients.

3. Whisk together the flour, sugar, baking powder, and salt in a large bowl. Whisk the cream into the sage butter (the butter might solidify a little when you do this—no worries) and then pour over the flour mixture. Stir with a flexible spatula until a shaggy dough forms.

4. Transfer the dough to the prepared baking sheet and, using your hands, gently shape it into a 6-inch round. The dough will look a little shiny and feel a little greasy from the melted butter—this is totally fine. Slice the round into eight wedges, as you would a pizza, with a bench scraper or chef's knife, and evenly space the scones on the sheet. Brush them with the egg wash and place a single sage leaf on top of each.

5. Bake for 17 to 20 minutes, until the tops and bottoms of the scones are nicely browned. Remove from the oven and let the scones cool on the baking sheet for about 5 minutes before serving with softened salted butter.

Pull-Apart Pimiento Cheese Scones

MAKES 8 SCONES
ACTIVE TIME: 15 MINUTES
BAKE TIME: 23 TO 28 MINUTES

2 cups (260 g) all-purpose flour, plus more for dusting

1½ tablespoons granulated sugar

1 tablespoon baking powder

1 teaspoon kosher salt

½ teaspoon freshly ground black pepper

¼ teaspoon cayenne pepper

1 teaspoon mustard powder

½ teaspoon garlic powder

½ teaspoon onion powder

½ cup (113 g) unsalted butter, cold and cubed

⅔ cup (127 g) well-drained, chopped jarred pimientos (about two 4-ounce jars)

1¾ cups (175 g) shredded extra-sharp Cheddar

⅔ cup (160 g) heavy cream, cold

1 teaspoon Worcestershire sauce

1 large egg, cold

The Ultimate Egg Wash (page 230)

Oh gosh, do I ever love pimiento cheese. I mean, it's made with cream cheese, mayo, Cheddar, and cute little tangy pimientos—what's not to love (particularly if you're me and mayo and cream cheese are your everything)? And said love runs deep: if I had had my way, the flavors of pimiento cheese would have been featured in every chapter of this book. The combo of Cheddar (orange, please!) and pimiento peppers looks and sounds like a savory bake's best friend, and it is truly fab and oh, so colorful in these pull-apart cuties. But in addition to the out-of-this-world flavor and appearance, these scones are also a texturally flaky home run, due to an easy stacking technique I learned from Claudia Fleming and Claire Saffitz while interviewing them each for my podcast. Thanks to Melissa Clark and Molly Yeh for inspiring the fun pull-apart assembly.

1. Heat the oven to 400°F. Have ready a baking sheet.

2. Whisk together the flour, sugar, baking powder, salt, black pepper, cayenne, mustard powder, and garlic and onion powders in a large bowl. Rub the butter into the flour mixture with your fingers until pea-size. Add the pimientos and cheese, and toss with your hands to combine. Whisk together the cream, Worcestershire, and egg in a 2-cup glass measuring cup, if you have one, or a medium bowl, and pour over the flour mixture. Gently stir with a flexible spatula just until no loose flour remains.

3. Turn out the dough onto a lightly floured piece of parchment paper. Pat it into a rectangle with the long side facing you. Cut the rectangle in half vertically with a bench scraper or chef's knife, and stack one half on top of the other. Rotate the stacked dough a quarter turn, pat it into a rectangle again, and repeat the cutting and stacking. Rotate, pat, cut, and stack once more, and then roughly shape the dough into an 8-inch round. Use the paper to lift the dough onto the baking sheet. Score the round with your bench scraper or chef's knife into eight wedges (as you would a pizza), cutting about two-thirds of the way through the dough, while keeping the bottom third attached. Brush the round with the egg wash.

4. Bake for 23 to 28 minutes, until the top and bottom of the "scone" is nicely browned. Remove from the oven and let cool on the baking sheet for about 10 minutes before serving, letting folks pull the scones apart themselves, for a real thrill.

"BLT" Scones

WITH BACON, LEMON, AND SUN-DRIED TOMATOES

Lemony, tender, salty, flaky, and moist, with loads of umami, these flavor bombs have a tiny bit of chew from the sun-dried tomatoes. Yes, you could add cheese to these, to great and tasty effect, but I wasn't sure you wanted cheese in *every* recipe in the book. Brushing the scones postbake with sun-dried tomato oil provides a little shine and an extra boost of tomato flavor. These will truly give your BLT sammy a run for its money (and, yes, the scones will win every time).

MAKES 8 SCONES
ACTIVE TIME: 15 MINUTES
BAKE TIME: 20 TO 23 MINUTES

3 tablespoons lemon zest

1½ tablespoons granulated sugar

2 cups (260 g) all-purpose flour, plus more for dusting

1 tablespoon baking powder

1 teaspoon kosher salt

½ teaspoon mustard powder

½ teaspoon freshly ground black pepper

One batch Fast and Dirty (Not Literally) Bacon (page 241)

⅔ cup (100 g) sun-dried tomatoes in oil, chopped finely

2 tablespoons sun-dried tomato oil, plus more for brushing postbake

1 cup (240 g) heavy cream

The Ultimate Egg Wash (page 230)

Flaky sea salt for sprinkling

1. Heat the oven to 400°F. Line a baking sheet with parchment paper.

2. Rub the zest into the sugar, with your fingers, in a large bowl. Whisk in the flour, baking powder, salt, mustard powder, and pepper. Toss in the crispy bacon bits and tomatoes with your hands. Whisk the tomato oil into the cream in a small bowl and pour over the flour mixture. Stir with a flexible spatula until a shaggy dough forms.

3. Turn out the dough onto a lightly floured work surface. Roughly shape the slightly crumbly dough into a 7-inch round with your hands and slice into eight wedges (as you would a pizza), with a bench scraper or chef's knife. Evenly space the scones on the prepared baking sheet, brush with the egg wash, and sprinkle with flaky salt.

4. Bake for about 20 to 23 minutes, until the tops and bottoms of the scones are nicely browned. Remove from the oven and immediately brush each scone with additional tomato oil. Let the scones cool on the baking sheet for about 5 minutes before serving.

Chorizo, Manchego, and Date Scones

MAKES 10 SCONES
ACTIVE TIME: 15 MINUTES
BAKE TIME: 17 TO 20 MINUTES

½ cup (113 g) unsalted
    butter, cubed
2 teaspoons smoked paprika
2 cups (260 g) all-purpose flour
1½ tablespoons granulated
    sugar
1 tablespoon baking powder
¼ teaspoon baking soda
1 teaspoon kosher salt
1 cup (85 g) deli or sandwich
    meat–style thinly sliced
    Spanish chorizo, cut into
    ½-inch pieces
1½ cups (150 g) shredded
    Manchego
¾ cup (109 g) pitted and
    coarsely chopped
    Medjool dates
½ cup (113 g) buttermilk, cold
The Ultimate Egg Wash
    (page 230)
Softened salted butter

These are a fab flavor bomb of a scone. Flaky and moist, with a warm, smoky flavor, the punchy chorizo bits and melty cheese pockets are the perfect foil to the chunks of caramelized dates: sweet and salty heaven, in other words. Manchego is a firm, Spanish, and very buttery sheep's milk cheese that marries beautifully with meat and dried fruit and is easy to find in the grocery store (it also plays well with Spanish Marcona almonds, which replace the chorizo in the vegetarian variation). Dried and cured, deli-style thinly sliced Spanish chorizo is best here (not Mexican chorizo, which is raw). If you can't find deli style, you can use the log-style Spanish chorizo, sliced into thin coins and chopped into ¼-inch pieces. And FYI: my photo team went bananas for these at the shoot, just sayin'.

1. Heat the oven to 400°F. Line a baking sheet with parchment paper.

2. Melt the butter, along with the smoked paprika, either in a 2-cup glass measuring cup in a microwave on HIGH or in a small saucepan on the stovetop. Set aside to infuse while you assemble the remaining ingredients.

3. Whisk together the flour, sugar, baking powder, baking soda, and salt in a large bowl. Toss in the chorizo, cheese, and dates and mix with your hands. Whisk the buttermilk into the paprika butter—it will curdle—don't worry. Pour the buttermilk mixture over the flour mixture and fold with a flexible spatula until a shaggy dough forms.

4. Scoop the dough into 10 balls, about a slightly rounded ⅓ cup each, using a portion scoop, if you have one, or a dry measuring cup. The dough is a bit crumbly—don't worry! Just use your hands to press any crumbly bits back into each ball. Dunk the tops and sides of the scones in the egg wash for optimal coverage and evenly place them on the prepared baking sheet.

5. Bake for 17 to 20 minutes, until the tops and bottoms of the scones are nicely browned. Remove from the oven and let the scones cool on the baking sheet for about 5 minutes before serving with loads of softened salted butter.

VARIATION

For Marcona, Manchego, and Date Scones, substitute ¾ cup (105 g) of coarsely chopped Marcona almonds for the chorizo.

Mini Irish Soda Bread Scones
WITH CHEDDAR AND THYME

MAKES 15 MINI SCONES

ACTIVE TIME: 15 MINUTES

BAKE TIME: 12 TO 16 MINUTES

1¾ cups (227 g) all-purpose flour

1½ tablespoons granulated sugar

¾ teaspoon baking soda

½ teaspoon kosher salt

½ teaspoon freshly ground black pepper

3 tablespoons chopped fresh thyme

1¼ cups (125 g) shredded aged Cheddar, plus more for sprinkling

¾ cups (170 g) buttermilk, plus a drizzle or two if dough is dry

The Ultimate Egg Wash (page 230)

My mother-in-law, always ahead of the curve, visited the Ballymaloe Cookery School, located on an organic farm in Ireland and run by the remarkable Darina Allen, many times over many years, and on each visit, a recipe "book" of all that the students had cooked and baked during their stay was gifted to them. Lucky enough to be the recipient of one such "book" (thank you, Nonnie!), I was inspired to make these soda bread *scones* in light of the fact that—yes, you guessed it—they are so darn easy. Mature Cheddar is what Balymaloe recommends, and who am I to argue with genius, so I used Kerrygold Dubliner here and sprinkled a bit on the scone tops prebake, to boot. These don't call for fat (butter or cream) as is traditional when soda bread making, but I added a little sugar to "season" the scones. I love the way these look when they are scooped into diminutive 2-tablespoon-ish balls, but if you prefer larger scones, be my jumbo-loving-scone guest (though you might need to add a few minutes to the bake time).

1. Heat the oven to 450°F. Line a baking sheet with parchment paper.

2. Whisk together the flour, sugar, baking soda, salt, pepper, thyme, and cheese in a large bowl. Pour in the buttermilk and mix with a flexible spatula, or your hands, until the dough just comes together and there are no more patches of dry flour. Sprinkle an additional tablespoon or so of buttermilk over the dry bits in the bowl, if need be, and then incorporate them into the dough. The dough will be sticky. Scoop 15 balls of dough (a generous 2 tablespoons each), with a portion scoop, if you have one, or with measuring spoons.

3. Dunk the top and sides of the scones in the egg wash for optimal coverage, evenly space them on the prepared baking sheet and sprinkle each generously with extra Cheddar.

4. Place the baking sheet in the oven and immediately lower the heat to 400°F. Bake for 12 to 16 minutes, until nicely browned and, when you tap the bottom of a scone, it sounds hollow. Remove from the oven and let the scones cool on the baking sheet for about 5 minutes before serving.

CHAPTER 2

The Sliceables (aka Savory Loaves and Snacking "Breads")

I feel the same way about my sliceables (savory tea loaves and snacking "breads") as I do my muffins, scones, and biscuits: could one really write a book of simple savory baked goods without them? Sliceables, as you've likely gathered, are essentially like savory muffins but baked in loaf tins and 8-by-8-inch square baking pans. They are delightful served just as they are, but many would also be lovely spread with butter or cream cheese or topped with cheese and toasted (some melty sharp Cheddar with a little spicy mustard on a slice of "Matty's" Nutty Seed Brown Bread (page 67) is my idea of heaven). Or, try a slice of "Pesto" Snacking "Bread" with Mozzarella (page 71) alongside Sunday sauce and meatballs, or for a tasty lunch with a big green salad tossed with a tangy vinaigrette. For brunch, skip the bagels and make an Everything Bagel and Cream Cheese Snacking "Bread" (page 68) instead. Serve it with smoked salmon and thinly sliced red onions, and make sure my invite doesn't get lost in the mail.

Pro Tips, Fun Facts, and Storing/Reheating Instructions

- And speaking of my Everything Bagel and Cream Cheese Snacking "Bread," there's a really tasty variation with za'atar, feta, and lemon (page 69); and if you want to **make your own za'atar**, whisk together 2 tablespoons of dried marjoram, 1 tablespoon of dried thyme, and 2 tablespoons of dried oregano. You can also use this homemade version when you whip up the Tomato Za'atar Galette with Onion and Cheese (page 124).

- "Snacking" *bread* is my cute little name for a **savory snacking cake**. Texturally it's bouncier, *cakier*, and less chewy than actual bread. Think: tea loaf in a cake pan.

TO STORE/REHEAT: Sliceables are best eaten the day they are made, fresh from the oven and still warm, but will last, tightly wrapped, for up to 3 days in the refrigerator if they have cheese, and on the counter if they do not—though the Ballymaloe Rosemary Onion Focaccia (page 79) and Whole Wheat Buttermilk Soda Bread (page 76) do well on the counter only overnight. Sliceables can be frozen for up to a month; but consider slicing before doing so to streamline enjoying one slice at a time.

Reheat room-temperature sliceables, wrapped in foil, in a 300°F oven until warm, about 10 minutes. And not to throw too much at you here, but the loaves and the soda bread can also be sliced and toasted, rather than warmed in the oven.

Why, Bonjour! A Loaf

MAKES ONE 8½-BY-4½-INCH LOAF

ACTIVE TIME: 15 MINUTES

BAKE TIME: 40 TO 45 MINUTES

1¼ cups (125 g) finely grated Parmesan, divided

½ cup (113 g) unsalted butter

1 generous tablespoon minced garlic (about 4 cloves)

½ cup (30 g) finely chopped mixed fresh herbs, such as parsley, chives, and tarragon

3 tablespoons granulated sugar

2 large eggs

1 cup (240 g) full-fat yogurt (not Greek)

1¾ teaspoons baking powder

¼ teaspoon baking soda

1 teaspoon kosher salt

½ teaspoon red pepper flakes

1 teaspoon mustard powder

½ teaspoon freshly ground black pepper

1¾ cups (227 g) all-purpose flour

Why add a French word to the title of this tea bread, you might be asking. Well, this garlicky bread of Parmesan and herbs gives me (and hopefully you) all the sophisticated Parisian vibes, as it is my version of a *salé*—a savory French loaf cake. I like to dust the interior of the pan with Parmesan for an extra cheesy finish, and to soak the garlic in the melted butter while I chop the herbs (for maximum garlicky flavor). And, yes: I do use jarred minced garlic here and I'm not ashamed to tell you (okay, maybe I'm a little ashamed?). A mixture of soft (think: parsley) and woody (think: tarragon) herbs is best.

1. Heat the oven to 350°F. Grease an 8½-by-4½-inch loaf pan with cooking spray or softened unsalted butter. Coat the bottom and sides of the pan with ¼ cup (25 g) of the Parmesan.

2. Melt the butter together with the minced garlic, either in a 2-cup glass measuring cup, if you have one, or a glass bowl in a microwave on HIGH, in three 30-second bursts, or in a small saucepan on the stovetop. Set aside to infuse while you assemble the remaining ingredients.

3. Rub the herbs into the sugar, with your fingers, in a large bowl. Whisk in the garlic and melted butter mixture, and then the eggs, one at a time. Vigorously whisk in the yogurt, then the baking powder, and finally the baking soda, followed by the salt, red pepper flakes, mustard powder, and black pepper. Gently fold in the flour and remaining cup of Parmesan just until the last streak of flour disappears. Transfer the batter to the prepared pan and smooth the top.

4. Bake for 40 to 45 minutes, until a wooden skewer inserted in the center comes out with a moist crumb or two. Remove from the oven and let cool until you can touch the pan without burning yourself. Then, invert the loaf onto a serving platter. Serve warm or at room temperature with French butter, if you have it (joke).

Savory Pumpkin Loaf
WITH SALTY PEPITAS

MAKES ONE 8½-BY-4½-INCH
LOAF
ACTIVE TIME: 10 MINUTES
BAKE TIME: 53 TO 58 MINUTES

½ cup (100 g) vegetable oil

⅔ cup (133 g) packed light
brown sugar

1 large egg

¾ teaspoon baking soda

½ teaspoon baking powder

½ teaspoon ground cumin

½ teaspoon ground coriander

¼ teaspoon ground turmeric

¼ teaspoon cayenne pepper

1 teaspoon kosher salt

½ teaspoon freshly ground
black pepper

1 scant cup (213 g) pure
pumpkin puree (about half
of a 15-ounce can)

⅓ cup (78 g) water

1½ cups (195 g) all-purpose flour

¼ cup (35 g) roasted and
salted pumpkin seeds
(aka pepitas)

Softened cream cheese
for serving

Flaky sea salt for sprinkling

Who knew a moist, slightly spicy, seed-topped pumpkin loaf could be this wildly delicious? The spices, especially the cayenne and cumin, round out the pumpkin's fruitiness, transforming an ever-popular vegetal sweet loaf into something decidedly savory. The pepitas add wonderful texture and color; and although they look best when sprinkled whole, if you chop them first, you get more even coverage and the loaf is easier to slice. For me it's a toss-up, as sometimes looks really *are* everything and a whole pepita–sprinkled loaf is my kind of everything.

1. Heat the oven to 350°F. Grease an 8½-by-4½-inch loaf pan with cooking spray. Line the bottom with a long sheet of parchment paper that extends up and over the two long sides of the pan.

2. Whisk together the oil, brown sugar, and egg in a large bowl. Vigorously whisk in the baking soda, then the baking powder, then the cumin, coriander, turmeric, cayenne, salt, and black pepper, and finally, the pumpkin and water. Gently fold in the flour with a flexible spatula just until the last streak disappears.

3. Transfer the batter to the prepared pan, smooth the top, and sprinkle with the pepitas, lightly pressing them down with your hands to adhere.

4. Bake for 53 to 58 minutes, rotating the pan at the halfway point, until a wooden skewer inserted in the center comes out with a moist crumb or two. Remove from the oven and let cool until you can easily lift the bread out of the pan by its parchment handles, about 20 minutes, running a knife around the edges if it resists. Let cool to room temperature before serving with softened cream cheese and flaky salt.

Cocktail Hour Loaf

MAKES ONE 8½-BY-4½-INCH LOAF
ACTIVE TIME: 15 MINUTES
BAKE TIME: 55 TO 60 MINUTES

½ cup (100 g) vegetable oil

3 tablespoons granulated sugar

2 large eggs

¾ cup (180 g) whole milk

1¾ teaspoons baking powder

1 teaspoon kosher salt

½ teaspoon garlic powder

¾ teaspoon mustard powder

¼ teaspoon cayenne pepper

½ teaspoon freshly ground black pepper

1½ cups (195 g) all-purpose flour

2 cups (200 g) shredded Swiss cheese, plus more for sprinkling

1 cup (145 g) drained small pimiento-stuffed olives, coarsely chopped, brine reserved

Sliced olives for decorating (optional)

Pimiento-stuffed green olives and melty Swiss cheese provide this loaf with loads o' dirty martini vibes circa the 1970s. And seeing as I adore pimiento cheese (see page 48 for why), it should come as no surprise that I also love pimiento-stuffed olives. The loaf's interior is wonderfully moist and the top a little crusty—both due to the cheese in and on this beauty. Sliced, she would make for an epic ham sandwich . . . or, my fave: mortadella (and the green pistachios in the mortadella would look so fantastic alongside the green of the olives, that now I'm thinking the loaf should be sliced into bite-size pieces and served with a piece of mortadella draped atop each one. Yum.) Don't forget to reserve your olive brine for a postbake brush and don't mind me as I slip into the kitchen to heat the oven and slice up that jar of olives I've been saving for cocktail hour (loaf).

1. Heat the oven to 350°F. Grease an 8½-by-4½-inch loaf pan with cooking spray. Line the bottom with a large sheet of parchment paper that extends up and over the two long sides of the pan.

2. Whisk together the oil and sugar in a large bowl. Whisk in the eggs, one at a time, and then the milk. Vigorously whisk in the baking powder and then the salt, garlic powder, mustard powder, cayenne, and black pepper. Gently fold in the flour, cheese, and olives with a flexible spatula just until the last streak of flour disappears.

3. Transfer the batter to the prepared pan, smooth the top, and sprinkle with additional cheese and sliced olives (if using).

4. Bake for 55 to 60 minutes, until a wooden skewer inserted in the center comes out with a moist crumb or two. Remove from the oven and very lightly brush the top of the loaf with some of the reserved olive brine. Let cool until you can easily lift the bread out of the pan by its parchment handles, about 20 minutes, running a knife around the edges if it resists. Serve warm or at room temperature with your favorite cocktail.

VARIATION

For French Onion Soup Bread, substitute onion powder for the garlic powder; ¾ teaspoon of dried thyme for the cayenne pepper; Quickest (Yet Tastiest) Caramelized Onions (page 237), chopped roughly, for the pimiento-stuffed olives; and olive oil for the olive brine, to brush postbake. Top the loaf prebake only with additional cheese.

"Matty's" Nutty Seed Brown Bread

MAKES ONE
8½-BY-4½-INCH LOAF
ACTIVE TIME: 10 MINUTES
BAKE TIME: 40 TO 45 MINUTES

¼ cup (50 g) olive oil
1 large egg
1 cup (230 g) full-fat sour cream
¼ cup (59 g) molasses
1½ teaspoons baking powder
½ teaspoon baking soda
1 teaspoon kosher salt
1 cup (100 g) toasted walnuts, chopped finely
½ cup (70 g) sunflower seeds, toasted, plus more untoasted seeds for sprinkling
¼ cup (35 g) black sesame seeds, plus more for sprinkling
¼ cup (35 g) white sesame seeds, plus more for sprinkling
1 cup (120 g) whole wheat flour
1 cup (130 g) all-purpose flour
Flaky sea salt for sprinkling

My husband, Matt, is a big fan of Mary's Gone Crackers Super Seed Crackers (if you know, you know) and of this bread. And although he doesn't *love* it when I call him "Matty," I couldn't resist naming this seeded loaf after him, while simultaneously giving a nod to his favorite cracker. The bread is petite and, with the addition of whole wheat flour, wonderfully wholesome. I love it toasted and slathered in softened salted butter (but what else is new?) and it is also great with a soft cheese, such as goat, or served just like its namesake crackers: with a cheese plate.

1. Heat the oven to 350°F. Grease an 8½-by-4½-inch loaf pan with cooking spray. Line the bottom with a long sheet of parchment paper that extends up and over the two long sides of the pan.

2. Whisk together the oil, egg, sour cream, and molasses in a large bowl. Vigorously whisk in the baking powder, then the baking soda, and then the salt, walnuts, and all of the seeds. Fold in the flours with a flexible spatula just until the last streak of flour disappear. The batter will be superthick and almost doughlike. Scrape it into the prepared pan, smooth the top, and sprinkle with the additional seeds and the flaky salt, firmly pressing them down with your hands to adhere.

3. Bake for 40 to 45 minutes, rotating at the halfway point, until a wooden skewer inserted in the center comes out with a moist crumb or two. Remove from the oven and let cool until you can easily lift the bread out of the pan by its parchment handles, about 20 minutes, running a knife around the edges if it resists. Serve warm, at room temperature, or toasted with whatever floats your boat—soft cheese, hard cheese, butter and jam . . .

Everything Bagel and Cream Cheese Snacking "Bread"

I don't know what to say, friends, except that a snacking bread with capers, cream cheese pockets, and copious amounts of everything bagel spice blend is my idea of a VERY good time. The softness of the bread coupled with the creaminess of the cheese, the tang from the capers, the sharpness from the flaked garlic and dried minced onion, and the crunch from the poppy seeds is just *everything* (pun intended) that your mouth has been asking for.

MAKES ONE 8-INCH SQUARE BREAD
ACTIVE TIME: 15 MINUTES
BAKE TIME: 30 TO 35 MINUTES

6 ounces (170 g) full-fat cream cheese, cold

2 tablespoons poppy seeds or black sesame seeds

1 tablespoon plus 1 teaspoon sesame seeds

1 tablespoon plus 1 teaspoon dried garlic flakes

1 tablespoon plus 1 teaspoon dried minced onion

2 generous teaspoons flaky sea salt

½ cup (113 g) unsalted butter, melted and cooled slightly

3 tablespoons granulated sugar

2 large eggs

¾ cup (170 g) buttermilk

1½ teaspoons baking powder

¼ teaspoon baking soda

½ cup (80 g) drained capers in brine

1½ cups (195 g) all-purpose flour

1. Heat the oven to 350°F. Grease an 8-inch square baking pan with cooking spray. Line the pan with a long piece of parchment paper that extends up and over two opposite sides of the pan.

2. Cut the cream cheese into 24 portions, about 1½ teaspoons each, place them on a plate, and chill in the refrigerator. Whisk together the poppy and sesame seeds, dried garlic and onion, and flaky salt (the "everything" mixture) in a small bowl and set aside. Whisk together the melted butter and sugar in a large bowl. Whisk in the eggs, one at a time, and then the buttermilk. Vigorously whisk in the baking powder, then the baking soda, and then the "everything" mixture, reserving a tablespoon of it to sprinkle on the top of the bread. Fold in the cold cream cheese portions (but do so gently so the cream cheese doesn't blend into the batter), capers, and flour with a flexible spatula, just until the last streak of flour disappears. Transfer the batter to the prepared pan, smooth the top, and sprinkle with the reserved "everything" mixture.

3. Bake for 30 to 35 minutes, until a wooden skewer inserted in the center comes out with a moist crumb or two. Remove from the oven and let cool until you can easily lift the bread out of the pan by its parchment handles, about 10 minutes, running a knife around the edges if it resists. Serve warm with extra cream cheese, red onions, and lox.

For Za'atar, Feta, and Lemon Snacking "Bread," omit the capers and, in place of the cream cheese, substitute 6 ounces (170 g) of Greek feta cheese, cut into ½- to ¾-inch cubes. Substitute ½ cup (100 g) of olive oil for the melted butter. In a large bowl, rub 2 tablespoons of lemon zest into the sugar, along with ½ teaspoon of kosher salt, before adding the oil. Substitute 3 tablespoons of za'atar spice blend for the sesame seeds, garlic flakes, minced onion, and flaky sea salt, adding it to the batter in place of the "everything" mixture. Combine an additional 1½ tablespoons of za'atar with 2½ tablespoons of olive oil and brush over the top of the bread before baking.

"Pesto" Snacking "Bread"
WITH MOZZARELLA

When I originally conceived of a pesto snacking bread, I pictured it swirled with actual pesto—like a pesto ribbon. But when that proved trickier than I anticipated, I changed course and developed a bread with all of pesto's *ingredients*, but deconstructed. Plus, I just had to throw in my favorite cheese: mozzarella (which creates the most perfect melty nooks and crannies). The bread is chock-full of ingredients that lend it its salty and herby flavor, as well as its slightly chewy and thick (almost biscuitlike) texture. Serve slices to the pesto and mozzie lovers in your life (and I hope there are many).

MAKES ONE 8-INCH SQUARE BREAD

ACTIVE TIME: 15 MINUTES

BAKE TIME: 30 TO 35 MINUTES

½ cup (100 g) olive oil, plus more for brushing postbake

3 tablespoons granulated sugar

2 large eggs

½ cup (120 g) whole milk

2 teaspoons baking powder

1 teaspoon kosher salt

½ teaspoon freshly ground black pepper

¾ teaspoon red pepper flakes

1 teaspoon garlic powder

1½ cups (195 g) all-purpose flour

1 cup (30 g) roughly chopped fresh basil

½ cup (58 g) pine nuts, toasted

1 cup (100 g) finely grated Parmesan

1 cup (140 g) cubed low-moisture whole-milk mozzarella (¼- to ½-inch cubes)

1. Heat the oven to 350°F. Grease an 8-inch square baking pan with cooking spray. Line the pan with a long piece of parchment paper that extends up and over two opposite sides of the pan.

2. Whisk together the oil and sugar in a large bowl. Whisk in the eggs, one at a time, and then the milk. Vigorously whisk in the baking powder, and then the salt, black pepper, red pepper flakes, and garlic powder. Fold in the flour, basil, pine nuts, Parmesan, and mozzarella with a flexible spatula, just until the last streak of flour disappears. Transfer the batter—it will be very thick—to the prepared pan and smooth it out.

3. Bake for 30 to 35 minutes, until a wooden skewer inserted in the center comes out with a moist crumb or two. Remove from the oven and immediately lightly brush the top of the bread with olive oil. Let cool until you can easily lift the bread out of the pan by its parchment handles, about 10 minutes, running a knife around the edges if it resists. Serve warm with Baked Spaghetti "Pie" with Cheesy Marinara (page 123).

Hot Honey-Butter Glazed Cornbread

Sweet, hot, moist, and toothsome, this utterly gorgeous and flavorful bread is literally the stuff of which cornbread dreams are made. I was first turned onto honey butter–soaked cornbread at one of my favorite neighborhood spots, Hometown, Billy Durney's fabulous barbecue joint. Hometown's slices are huge and generously saturated with honey butter. And once I learned how easy it is to make hot honey—one of my all-time fave condiments—from scratch, I knew I had a *hot* honey-butter cornbread in my future. Soaking your cornbread with copious amounts of honey butter postbake, à la Hometown, is the pro move we all need to be making.

MAKES ONE 8-INCH ROUND
CORNBREAD
ACTIVE TIME: 10 MINUTES
BAKE TIME: 25 TO 30 MINUTES

BREAD

1¼ cups (162 g) all-purpose flour

1 cup (145 g) medium-grind
  cornmeal

2 teaspoons baking powder

¼ teaspoon baking soda

1 teaspoon kosher salt

½ cup (100 g) packed light
  brown sugar

1 cup (227 g) buttermilk

¼ cup (56 g) unsalted butter,
  melted and cooled slightly

¼ cup (50 g) vegetable oil

2 large eggs

GLAZE

¼ cup (84 g) honey

¼ cup (56 g) unsalted butter

½ teaspoon red pepper flakes

2 teaspoons hot sauce, such
  as Cholula or Frank's brand,
  or to taste

1. Heat the oven to 375°F. Grease an 8-inch round cake pan with cooking spray and line the bottom with parchment paper.

2. Whisk together the flour, cornmeal, baking powder, baking soda, salt, and brown sugar in a large bowl. In a 2-cup glass measuring cup, if you have one, or a medium bowl, whisk together the buttermilk, melted butter, oil, and eggs. Pour the buttermilk mixture over the flour mixture, and gently fold with a flexible spatula to combine just until the last streak of flour disappears.

3. Scrape the batter into the prepared pan and smooth the top.

4. Bake for 25 to 30 minutes, until a wooden skewer inserted in the center comes out with a moist crumb or two.

5. While the cornbread bakes, make the glaze: Combine the honey, butter, red pepper flakes, and hot sauce in a small saucepan and bring to a simmer over medium heat. Remove the cornbread from the oven and immediately run a butter knife around the edge of the pan. Pour the glaze over the hot cornbread, coaxing it with the back of a spoon, if needed, to evenly cover the surface. Let it sit for 5 to 7 minutes until the glaze is completely absorbed. Serve wedges warm, straight from the pan.

Kathy's Old-Fashioned Cracklin' Bread

MAKES ONE 8-INCH SQUARE
CORNBREAD
ACTIVE TIME: 20 MINUTES
BAKE TIME: ABOUT 25 MINUTES

1½ cups (218 g) medium-grind
    cornmeal
½ cup (65 g) all-purpose flour
¼ cup (50 g) granulated sugar
1 teaspoon baking powder
½ teaspoon baking soda
1 teaspoon kosher salt
½ teaspoon freshly ground
    black pepper
One batch Fast and Dirty (Not
    Literally) Bacon (page 241),
    fat reserved (see below)
1 cup (100 g) shredded
    Cheddar
3 tablespoons reserved bacon
    fat, at room temperature
    but still pourable (if
    cooking bacon yields less
    fat, make up the difference
    with vegetable oil)
3 tablespoons vegetable oil
2 large eggs
1⅓ cups (303 g) buttermilk
Softened salted butter
    for serving

I discovered a recipe for cracklin' bread in an old cookbook that my pal Kathy gifted me (Kathy's an excellent home baker and grandmother and is extremely generous with her recipe collection). Cracklin' bread is cornbread generously studded with small crispy bits of bacon. Here, for even smokier, salty flavor, some of the fat is also incorporated into the batter. Cheese is not traditional, but I love it with the bacon and corn. The crumb here is compact and toothsome—due to the ratio of cornmeal to flour—and the bread itself is moist and rich. Caroline, my North Floridian recipe tester and a cornbread aficionado, said "it's one of the best" (in case you were on the fence).

1. Heat the oven to 425°F. Grease an 8-inch square baking pan with cooking spray. Line the pan with a long piece of parchment paper that extends up and over two opposite sides of the pan.

2. Whisk together the cornmeal, flour, sugar, baking powder, baking soda, salt, and pepper in a large bowl, then whisk in the crispy bacon bits and cheese. In a 4-cup glass measuring cup, if you have one, or a large bowl, whisk together the bacon fat, oil, eggs, and buttermilk. Pour the buttermilk mixture over the cornmeal mixture and, using a flexible spatula, gently fold to combine just until the last streak of flour disappears. Scrape the batter into the prepared pan and smooth the top.

3. Bake for about 25 minutes, or until lightly browned and a wooden skewer inserted in the center comes out with a moist crumb or two. Remove from the oven and let cool until you can easily lift the bread out of the pan by its parchment handles, about 10 minutes, running a knife around the edges if it resists. Serve warm with softened salted butter.

Whole Wheat Buttermilk Soda Bread
WITH PECANS

MAKES ONE 7-INCH BOULE
ACTIVE TIME: 5 MINUTES
BAKE TIME: ABOUT 35 MINUTES

1¾ cups (227 g)
    all-purpose flour

1¾ cups (210 g) whole
    wheat flour

3 tablespoons packed light
    brown sugar

1 teaspoon kosher salt

1½ teaspoons baking soda

1 teaspoon baking powder

1 cup (100 g) pecans, toasted
    and chopped coarsely

1½ cups (340 g) buttermilk, plus
    a drizzle or two if dough is
    dry, and more for brushing

First off, I adore soda bread because it has "easy-peasy baker" written all over it. I mean, a bread that comes together in minutes with pantry-friendly ingredients—including chemical leaveners—and bakes in less than an hour is exactly what the snackable baking doctor ordered. This particular soda bread calls for whole wheat flour, which adds wonderful nuttiness and color to the finished loaf. The toasted pecans add additional texture (and flavor) to the bread—and warm, sliced, and spread with salted butter, is exactly how I hope you'll consider enjoying it.

1. Heat the oven to 450°F. Line a baking sheet with parchment paper.

2. Whisk together the flours, brown sugar, salt, baking soda, baking powder, and pecans in a large bowl. Pour in the buttermilk and mix with a flexible spatula, or your hands, until the dough just comes together and there are no more patches of dry flour. Sprinkle an additional tablespoon or so of buttermilk over the dry bits in the bowl, if need be, and then incorporate them into the dough. The dough will be sticky. Give the dough a turn or two in the bowl to form it into a craggy ball. Place the dough on the prepared baking sheet and tuck the sides underneath to make a ball about 6 inches wide. Cut a large cross into the top of the bread with a small serrated or paring knife.

3. Brush the loaf with buttermilk, place it in the oven, and immediately lower the heat to 400°F.

4. Bake for about 35 minutes, or until nicely browned and, when you tap the bottom of the loaf, it sounds hollow. Remove from the oven and let cool for about 10 minutes before slicing and serving warm with whatever floats your soda bread boat.

Ballymaloe Rosemary Onion "Focaccia"

MAKES ONE 9-BY-13-INCH
BREAD
ACTIVE TIME: 10 MINUTES
BAKE TIME: ABOUT 15 MINUTES

Olive oil for greasing the pan,
    drizzling and brushing
3½ cups (455 g)
    all-purpose flour
3 tablespoons granulated sugar
1 teaspoon kosher salt
1½ teaspoons baking soda
1 teaspoon baking powder
1½ cups (340 g) buttermilk,
    plus a drizzle or two if
    dough is dry
1 tablespoon chopped
    fresh rosemary
A generous ⅓ cup (30 g) thinly
    sliced red onion
Flaky sea salt for sprinkling
Freshly ground black pepper
    for sprinkling
Red pepper flakes
    for sprinkling

VARIATION

For Rosemary, Olive, and
Parm "Focaccia," substitute
⅔ cup (96 g) of drained, pitted
olives, such as Castelve-
trano or Kalamata, coarsely
chopped, for the red onions.
After brushing with olive oil
postbake, sprinkle with finely
grated Parmesan.

Who knew you could make focaccia from the same dough you use to make—wait for it—Irish soda bread! Well, you can. Learned about this trick, hack, *genius* idea from a "book" of Ballymaloe Cookery School recipes gifted to me by my MIL, who traveled to Ireland repeatedly to take cooking classes at the school. Obviously, this is not a *yeasted* focaccia situation, since soda bread is leavened with chemical leaveners, but it very much *looks* like focaccia (for what that's worth) and is extremely snackable. The rosemary and onion topping, coupled with the olive oil, flaky salt, and red pepper flakes couldn't be simpler or more satisfying.

1. Heat the oven to 450°F. Generously brush a 9-by-13-inch pan with olive oil.

2. Whisk together the flour, sugar, salt, baking soda, and baking powder in a large bowl. Pour in the buttermilk and mix with a flexible spatula, or your hands, until the dough just comes together and there are no more patches of dry flour. Sprinkle an additional tablespoon or so of buttermilk over the dry bits in the bowl, if need be, and then incorporate them into the dough. The dough will be sticky.

3. Transfer the dough to the prepared baking pan and press it gently into the bottom. It should be able to reach all four corners of the pan. Dampen your hands, if necessary, and use your fingers to create the classic "dimpled" look of a focaccia. Drizzle with olive oil and brush to cover, making sure to dab some in the dimples. Shower the dough with the rosemary, dot with the red onion slices, and sprinkle with the flaky salt, black pepper, and red pepper flakes.

4. Bake for about 15 minutes, or until nicely browned and crisped. Remove from the oven and immediately slide the bread out of the pan and onto a large cooling rack, with the help of a metal spatula. Brush with more olive oil. Let cool briefly and serve warm.

CHAPTER 3

Toasty Handhelds

Toasty handhelds are just as delightfully scrumptious to eat as their name implies. Many are perfect for a picnic, where out-of-hand eating should be a prerequisite, while others are wonderfully buttery and flaky, due to store-bought puff pastry, and might do better out of hand at the breakfast nook or around the kitchen table. Popovers make an appearance in this chapter, as tearing into a freshly baked popover with your bare hands and slathering it with butter (you can use a knife for the slathering part), before shoving it in your mouth, is an experience worth having (and one with which I hope you will fall in love). And not sure there is a better easy-peasy, savory, handheld treat for brekkie than Jenny's Egg Puffs with Prosciutto Bottoms (page 84). Variations abound in this chapter, as satisfying ALL the toasty handheld cravings is a high priority.

Pro Tips, Fun Facts, and Storing/Reheating Instructions

- **Puff pastry purchased from the grocery store** is one of the most bang-for-the-buck baking products around. It tastes fantastic—I mean, buttery flakiness FTW every time—and looks incredible in every application. Like, "Oh, my gosh: I *made* that????" kind of incredible. It needs to be thawed before using, and I suggest thawing it overnight in the fridge or for 30 minutes or so on the counter, depending on the temperature of your kitchen.

- And pro tip here: Although some claim you need to flour your work surface before rolling out puff pastry, I have never found it to be necessary, as when you remove it from its packaging, you'll see that **the puff actually has a dusting of flour on one side**. As long as you place it, flour side down, on the counter when you go to roll it out, there shouldn't be any sticking, but work quickly to prevent the puff pastry from warming up and proving me wrong.

- **Hand pies are literally adorable**, and everyone prefers an individual little pie to a slice of a larger situation. So, yes, you're doing God's work when you assemble them and, also, everyone you share them with will literally love you forever for it, so there's that, too. However, we can all agree that **rolling out and assembling hand pies is a little time consuming**, there are no two ways about it. The dough itself is not the problem, however; in fact, it's your old friend: my easy-peasy Magic Melted Butter Pie Dough (page 233), from *Snackable Bakes*, which comes together in a heartbeat.

- And I have **a great tip for hand pie rolling:** divide the dough into the number of pies you're making and roll out each piece individually. I find this is easier than rolling out one large piece of dough and then cutting out the circles or squares you'll need for each pie, rerolling the cumbersome scraps, etc. Bottom line, peeps: Don't kill yourself trying to make perfect hand pies. In fact, do as I do (remember we're twinning here) and embrace their imperfect shape or the (scrumptious) filling that oozed out of one corner and proudly call them "rustic" or throw around the word "artisanal." No one will be the wiser.

TO STORE: Toasty handhelds are best eaten the day they are made, fresh from the oven and still warm, but will last for up to 3 days, tightly wrapped, in the refrigerator (save for the popovers—they will last just overnight on the counter); or in the freezer for up to a month.

TO REHEAT: Reheat room-temperature handhelds in a 300°F oven on a parchment-lined baking sheet until warm, about 10 minutes.

Jenny's Egg Puffs with Prosciutto Bottoms

MAKES 12 PUFFS
ACTIVE TIME: 5 MINUTES
BAKE TIME: 30 TO 35 MINUTES

12 slices prosciutto
4 large eggs, lightly beaten
½ cup (120 g) whole milk
¼ cup (56 g) unsalted butter, melted and cooled slightly
½ teaspoon baking powder
¼ teaspoon kosher salt
½ teaspoon freshly ground black pepper
¼ cup (33 g) all-purpose flour
2 cups (200 g) shredded Muenster, Monterey Jack, or low-moisture mozzarella
2 ounces (56 g) full-fat cream cheese, cubed
1 cup (226 g) cottage cheese, 2% fat or higher

I've known Jenny since I was a little kid, as our parents are old friends, and Jenny makes a mean cheesy egg situation that I am obsessed with. I love that it calls for Muenster cheese *and* cottage cheese *and* cream cheese. And I also love that I thought to make said situation muffin-sized and to line each cavity with a slice of prosciutto. But if you're not a meat-eater, you can bake them in cupcake liners for a truly on the go packable/portable snack experience; or, bake them directly in the greased tin for an extra-crispy bottom. Go to town with green chiles, chives (as seen here), herbs, bacon bits, etc.

1. Heat the oven to 350°F. Generously grease a 12-well muffin tin with cooking spray. Line each well with a slice of prosciutto, folding it to make it snugly fit the bottom and sides of each cavity.

2. Whisk together the eggs, milk, and melted butter in a large bowl. Sprinkle the baking powder, salt, and pepper over the egg mixture and whisk to combine. Whisk in the flour and then the Muenster, cream cheese, and cottage cheese. Evenly pour the batter into the prosciutto-lined wells of the prepared tin; each will be pretty full.

3. Bake for 30 to 35 minutes, rotating at the halfway point, until a wooden skewer inserted in the center comes out clean.

4. Remove the tin from the oven and let cool briefly on a wire rack before running a knife around the edge of the muffin wells and removing the egg puffs. Let cool for at least 10 minutes and serve warm or room temperature.

Sour Cherry, Goat Cheese, and Rosemary Danish

MAKES 8 DANISH
ACTIVE TIME: 10 MINUTES
BAKE TIME: ABOUT 25 MINUTES

1 large egg, lightly beaten

8 ounces (227 g) goat cheese, at room temperature

2 ounces (56 g) full-fat cream cheese, at room temperature

¾ teaspoon kosher salt

½ teaspoon freshly ground black pepper

2 sheets (17.3 ounces) store-bought frozen puff pastry, thawed

½ cup (160 g) sour cherry spread, or any thick jam you love

Scant 2 teaspoons chopped fresh rosemary

The Ultimate Egg Wash (page 230)

Flaky sea salt for sprinkling

Store-bought puff pastry and I are in a relatively new relationship. Like, prior to writing this cookbook, I'd really never used it before, and wow—am I ever in love (and am hoping the feeling is mutual). Making Danish with puff pastry has become my idea of a baking home run (easy, delicious, special—you get it). I added a bit of cream cheese to the goat cheese here, for a little tangy flavor and also to help with spreadability (learned this trick from *America's Test Kitchen*). Try to use sour cherry spread (such as Divina or Dalmatia brand), as opposed to sour cherry jam, as the jam will leak while baking.

1. Heat the oven to 400°F. Line two baking sheets with parchment paper.

2. Combine the egg, goat cheese, cream cheese, salt, and pepper in a medium bowl, using a fork.

3. Place one sheet of the puff pastry in the refrigerator and the other on a cutting board, flour side down, and roll it out just a bit to soften the seams. Cut the pastry into four equal-size squares with a pizza cutter, if you have one, or a chef's knife. Repeat with the other sheet of puff pastry. Place four squares on each prepared baking sheet and divide the goat cheese mixture equally among them (about 2 heaping tablespoons per Danish). Spread the mixture over each square, leaving about a ½-inch cheese-free border. Spoon a tablespoon (about 20 g) of jam onto the center of the cheese and sprinkle with rosemary. Brush the borders of the squares with egg wash.

4. Bake for about 25 minutes, rotating the sheets at the halfway point and swapping their placement in the oven, until the edges are puffed, browned, and crispy. Remove from the oven, sprinkle with flaky salt, let cool for about 10 minutes, and serve warm or at room temperature.

Ricotta and Onion "Puff" Tarts

MAKES 8 PUFF TARTS
ACTIVE TIME: 10 MINUTES
BAKE TIME: 20 TO 25 MINUTES

1½ cups (339 g) ricotta

¼ cup plus 2 tablespoons (37 g) finely grated Parmesan

¾ teaspoon kosher salt

½ teaspoon freshly ground black pepper

¼ teaspoon red pepper flakes, or to taste

½ teaspoon onion powder

½ teaspoon garlic powder

2 sheets (17.3 ounces) store-bought frozen puff pastry, thawed

One batch Quickest (Yet Tastiest) Caramelized Onions (page 237)

The Ultimate Egg Wash (page 230)

Pudgy, savory ~~pop~~ puff tarts with creamy ricotta, slightly sweet, caramelized onions, and a little kick from red pepper flakes are the little handheld treats you did not know you were missing. The recipe calls for my (brand-new) one true love, store-bought puff pastry, which means these could not be easier or faster to assemble. And although you might think caramelized onions require a long, slow cook, I've got a hack (see page 237) that is going to blow your mind.

1. Heat the oven to 400°F. Line a baking sheet with parchment paper.

2. Combine the ricotta, Parmesan, salt, black pepper, red pepper flakes, and onion and garlic powders in a medium bowl, using a fork.

3. Place one sheet of the puff pastry in the refrigerator and the other on a cutting board, flour side down, and roll it out just a bit to soften the seams. Cut the pastry into four equal-size squares with a pizza cutter, if you have one, or a sharp chef's knife. Brush the edges of the squares with the egg wash. Place 2 tablespoons of the cheese mixture and 1 tablespoon of the onions on one half of each square and fold the pastry over the filling. Seal the edges with your fingers. Place the puff tarts on the prepared baking sheet and use the tines of a fork to further seal the edges. Cut three small diagonal slits on top of each with a sharp paring knife and brush with additional egg wash. Repeat with the other sheet of puff pastry, making sure all the tarts are equally spaced on the baking sheet. You'll have some ricotta and a few onions leftover—spread the cheese on some crackers and top with the onions.

4. Bake the tarts for 20 to 25 minutes, rotating at the halfway point, until puffed, browned, and crispy—if they leak a tiny bit, no worries: rustic is in. Remove from the oven, let cool for about 10 minutes, and serve warm or at room temperature.

Baby Ham and Cheese "Croissants"

MAKES 12

ACTIVE TIME: 15 MINUTES

BAKE TIME: 20 TO 25 MINUTES

1 sheet (8.6 ounces) store-bought frozen puff pastry, thawed

2 tablespoons yellow or brown prepared mustard, you choose

3 ounces (85 g) Gruyère, grated

4 to 6 slices deli ham

The Ultimate Egg Wash (page 230)

Sesame seeds for sprinkling (optional)

VARIATION

For Cheesy Olive "Croissants," replace the ham with ¼ cup (65 g) of tapenade, spreading it over the mustard before adding the cheese.

I mean, these "babies" are just too adorbs for words. Reading the directions extra carefully to understand exactly how to shape these cuties is not a bad idea, but they're actually a cinch to assemble. And the mustard? Wouldn't suggest sleeping on it. To me, a ham and cheese croissant is just the perfect savory breakfast or lunchtime treat—and, of course, the beauty of eating little ones, is that you get to eat a lot.

1. Heat the oven to 400°F. Line a baking sheet with parchment paper.

2. Place the puff pastry on a cutting board, flour side down, and roll it out just a bit to soften the seams. Spread the mustard over the pastry, evenly sprinkle with the cheese, and press the cheese lightly to adhere it to the mustard. Using a pizza cutter, if you have one, or a chef's knife, cut the pastry in half vertically and then cut each half vertically into thirds, creating six long skinny rectangles. Cut each rectangle in half on the diagonal, creating 12 long, skinny triangles.

3. Position the triangles on the cutting board so the shortest side of each is closest to you and the point or tip is farthest from you. Cut the ham slices into triangles that snugly fit on the puff-angles (joke—puff *tri*angles). Begin rolling up the triangles from the short end toward the tip, ending with the tip on the bottom of the croissant. Evenly space the croissants on the prepared baking sheet, brush with egg wash, and sprinkle with sesame seeds (if using).

4. Bake the croissants for 20 to 25 minutes, rotating at the halfway point, until puffed, browned, and crispy. Remove from the oven, let cool for at least 10 minutes, and serve warm or at room temperature.

Pom's Boxing Day Sausage Rolls

My friend Pom always serves mini sausages around Christmas and she also makes a mean braised fennel. I'm, of course, crazy about both. Here, I've combined Pom's two "specialties" (though I'm using fennel *seeds*) with puff pastry. These rolls are buttery and salty with a little licorice kick and I hope they'll do Pom proud.

MAKES 12 ROLLS
ACTIVE TIME: 10 MINUTES
BAKE TIME: 20 TO 25 MINUTES

½ pound (227 g) raw bulk pork sausage or links, such as sweet Italian, or English bangers, if you can find them

1 large egg

¾ teaspoon kosher salt

½ teaspoon freshly ground black pepper

1 sheet (8.6 ounces) store-bought frozen puff pastry, thawed

2 tablespoons yellow or brown prepared mustard, you choose

The Ultimate Egg Wash (page 230)

Fennel seeds for sprinkling

1. Heat the oven to 400°F. Line a baking sheet with parchment paper.

2. Place the sausage (removed from the casings, if using links) in a large bowl. Add the egg, salt, and pepper, and use your hands or a flexible spatula to gently bring everything together—the sausage mixture will be wet and loose, but do not overmix.

3. Place the puff pastry on a cutting board, flour side down, and roll it out just a bit to soften the seams. Cut the pastry in half horizontally, so you have two rectangles with their long sides facing you. Spread 1 tablespoon of mustard over each rectangle, leaving a ½-inch bare border along the top, long-side of both. Brush the mustardless borders with egg wash. Divide the meat mixture equally between the rectangles, molding it into long logs that run along the bottom of each rectangle (the side without the egg wash). The logs should extend the entire length of the rectangle (they should be exposed at either end once rolled). Using your hands, shape the logs so they are about 1½ inches wide.

4. Firmly roll up the pastry from the bottom side of each rectangle to the top. Lightly pinch the seam closed. Brush, seam side down, with egg wash and sprinkle with fennel seeds. Cut each roll into six pieces and evenly space them on the prepared baking sheet.

5. Bake for 20 to 25 minutes, rotating at the halfway point, until puffed and browned. Don't overbake, or the filling will dry out. Remove from the oven, let cool for 10 minutes, and serve warm.

Grilled Cheese Sandwich Tart

MAKES 12 MINI SANDWICHES
ACTIVE TIME: 5 MINUTES
BAKE TIME: 22 TO 26 MINUTES

2 sheets (17.3 ounces) store-
    bought frozen puff
    pastry, thawed

Mayonnaise for brushing

18 slices American cheese,
    or other sliced and very
    melty cheese

¾ teaspoon dried oregano for
    sprinkling (optional)

The Ultimate Egg Wash
    (page 230)

VARIATION

For Turkey and Cheese Tart,
top the first layer of cheese
with eight slices of deli turkey
meat, cut or torn if necessary,
to cover the surface evenly;
then cover with the remaining cheese, and substitute a
sprinkling of Italian seasoning
for the oregano.

There's a whole low-/highbrow thing happening here that I adore, as this tart is both about the humble grilled *American* cheese sandwich AND the fancy deliciousness that is puff pastry. Zhoosh this up with mustard (my husband is all about mustard on his grilled cheese) and serve warm. And don't pass on actual bright orange American cheese—it's the most melty and cheese-pully (i.e., it's the best); or on the sprinkle of oregano (it comes courtesy of my pal Erik Kim's *New York Times* recipe for a grilled cheese sammy).

1. Heat the oven to 400°F. Have ready a baking sheet.

2. Place one sheet of the puff pastry in the refrigerator and the other on a sheet of parchment paper, flour side down, and roll it out just a bit to soften the seams. Transfer the parchment paper and puff pastry to the baking sheet. Brush the pastry with mayonnaise, leaving a ½-inch bare border around all sides. Place nine slices of cheese in three rows of three on top of the mayonnaise. Place the other nine slices directly on top of the first nine and sprinkle with oregano. Brush the exposed border with egg wash.

3. Place the other sheet of pastry, flour side down, on a cutting board, and roll it out just a bit to soften the seams. Lay it over the cheese. Trim the edges, if necessary, to make an even square and lightly press them down to seal. Score the top layer of pastry into 12 squares, cutting through to the cheese. Brush with egg wash, and dock the edges with a fork, pressing the tines through both layers of pastry, to prevent them from ris-ing up higher than the middle while baking.

4. Bake the tart for 22 to 26 minutes, until puffed, browned, and crispy. Remove from the oven and let cool for about 5 minutes, lightly pressing down on the edges if they have puffed up dra-matically taller than the middle. Slice along the scored lines and serve warm when the cheese is still gooey and stretchy.

Smash(ish) Burger Hand Pies
WITH CHEESE

MAKES 6 HAND PIES

ACTIVE TIME: 35 MINUTES

BAKE TIME: 20 MINUTES

PATTIES

1 pound (450 g) ground beef or ground turkey

Kosher salt for sprinkling

Freshly ground black pepper for sprinkling

HAND PIES

One batch Magic Melted Butter Pie Dough × 1½ (page 233)

Mayonnaise for brushing

1 cup plus 2 tablespoons (112 g) shredded cheese

The Ultimate Egg Wash (page 230)

A million years ago, *Bon Appétit* magazine published a recipe for smash burgers and I was surprised by how quickly they entered my family's dinner rotation. I'd always been a member of the thick and juicy burger camp and had no idea what a textural party in your mouth a skinny and crispy patty could throw. And, yes, it goes without saying that wrapping such a burger in pastry is a win-win all round. Here, the pastry-wrapped patties are a little more medium to medium-well than well done and are not quite as crispy, as a traditional smash. As for the cheese, American is a tiny bit too melty, so Cheddar is nice, or Swiss, or whatever you dig—and be sure to enjoy your burgers warm with all your fave condiments.

1. Heat the oven to 400°F. Line a baking sheet with parchment paper.

2. Divide and shape the ground meat into six 3½-inch-square patties, pressing them with your hands to flatten. Sprinkle both sides with salt and pepper.

3. Divide the pie dough into 12 pieces (about 55 g each) and cover with a clean dish towel to keep warm (the dough is easier to work with when warm). You'll be working with two pieces at a time. Roll out two pieces into 5-inch squares, picking them up and rotating them as you do so. You shouldn't need to flour your work surface, as the dough isn't very sticky, but you can roll the dough between two pieces of parchment for extra insurance. Brush both pieces with mayonnaise, leaving a ½-inch bare border around all sides of both pieces.

4. Sprinkle 1 tablespoon of cheese over the mayo, top it with a patty, and sprinkle an additional 2 tablespoons of cheese over the patty. Place the other piece of dough, mayo side down, over the cheese. Tightly roll the edges under to seal—it's nice to snugly package the meat in dough—then further seal them with a fork. Repeat with the remaining dough, patties, and cheese.

5. Transfer the pies to the prepared baking sheet, brush them with egg wash, and cut three small diagonal slits on the top of each with a sharp paring knife.

6. Bake for about 20 minutes, rotating at the halfway point, until the pies are golden on top and bottom. If using ground turkey, an instant-read thermometer inserted into the pies should read at least 160°F. Let rest for 10 to 15 minutes, so the juices reabsorb into the pies. Serve warm with ketchup and mustard and more mayonnaise on the side.

"Cuban" Hot Pockets

MAKES 6 HOT POCKETS
ACTIVE TIME: 35 MINUTES
BAKE TIME: 20 TO 25 MINUTES

One batch Magic Melted
   Butter Pie Dough × 1½
   (page 233)

FOR THE FILLING
12 slices Swiss cheese
6 slices boiled ham, such as
   Black Forest
6 slices Genoa salami (if slices
   are small, you may need 12)
3 to 6 large dill pickles,
   depending on size,
   sliced thinly
Kosher salt for sprinkling
Freshly ground black pepper
   for sprinkling
Mayonnaise for brushing
Yellow or brown prepared
   mustard for brushing
The Ultimate Egg Wash
   (page 230)

A pressed Cuban sandwich—with its melty cheese, salty pork loin, and vinegary pickles—is one of the best sammies I know. And so, it should come as no surprise that I tucked all that tastiness into a melted butter pie dough, hot pocket–esque hand pie in my savory baking book. I'm using ham here, instead of pork loin, and some salami (which is apparently what a Cuban sandwich made in Tampa includes). Pro tip: Buy presliced sandwich-style pickles (the long, flat ones) as they're very user-friendly when Cuban sandwich–making.

1. Heat the oven to 400°F. Line a baking sheet with parchment paper.

2. Divide the pie dough into 12 pieces (about 55 g each), and cover with a clean dish towel to keep warm (the dough is easier to work with when warm). You'll be working with two pieces at a time. Roll out two pieces into 5½-by-3½-inch rectangles, picking them up and rotating them as you do so. You shouldn't need to flour your work surface, as the dough isn't very sticky, but you can roll the dough between two pieces of parchment for extra insurance. Brush one rectangle with mayonnaise and the other with mustard, leaving a ½-inch bare border around all sides of both pieces.

3. Top one of the rectangles with a slice of cheese, then ham, salami, a couple of pickle slices, and another slice of cheese, trimming them to fit within the border. Sprinkle with salt and pepper. Brush the edges with egg wash and place the other rectangle on top, condiment side down. Press the edges together first with your fingertips, and then further seal them with a fork. Repeat with the remaining dough rectangles.

4. Transfer the pies to the prepared baking sheet, brush them with egg wash, and cut three small diagonal slits on the top of each with a sharp paring knife.

5. Bake for 20 to 25 minutes, rotating at the halfway point, until the pockets are golden on top and bottom. Remove from the oven and let cool for about 10 minutes before serving.

VARIATIONS

For "Reuben" Hot Pockets, substitute 12 slices of corned beef for the ham and salami, about 1 tablespoon of well-drained sauerkraut per pocket (¼ cup plus 2 tablespoons [about 50 g, total]) for the pickles, and spread Russian dressing on each half of the pie, instead of mayonnaise and mustard. To make the Russian dressing, whisk together 3 tablespoons of mayonnaise and 3 tablespoons of ketchup in a small bowl.

For "Pizza" Hot Pockets, substitute additional salami for the ham, provolone or mozzarella sandwich slices for the Swiss cheese, a few thin slices of jarred roasted red peppers for the pickles, and jarred marinara sauce for the mayonnaise and mustard, spreading a thin layer on each half of each pie. Sprinkle the tomato sauce with a pinch of dried oregano, dried basil, or red pepper flakes, if desired.

Oliver's Spinach and Feta Hand Pies

MAKES 9 HAND PIES
ACTIVE TIME: 30 MINUTES
BAKE TIME: 20 TO 25 MINUTES

FILLING

6 ounces (170 g) frozen
    spinach, defrosted and
    squeezed dry
5 ounces (142 g) feta
    cheese, crumbled
¼ teaspoon garlic powder
¼ teaspoon onion powder
¼ teaspoon mustard powder
⅛ teaspoon kosher salt
½ teaspoon freshly ground
    black pepper
¼ teaspoon freshly grated
    nutmeg
¼ teaspoon cayenne pepper
1 large egg, lightly beaten
1 tablespoon freshly squeezed
    lemon juice (from
    about ½ lemon)

HAND PIES

One batch Magic Melted
    Butter Pie Dough × 1
    (page 233)
Mayonnaise for brushing
Sesame seeds for
    sprinkling (optional)
The Ultimate Egg Wash
    (page 230)

When my older son, Oliver, was still stroller-bound (aka many years ago), he adored the triangular spinach and feta whole wheat pies from Damascus, a Middle Eastern bakery near our home. I'd push him around town feeling so virtuous that my kid snacked on whole wheat pies with spinach and tangy feta, all the while licking my Ben and Jerry's ice cream cone (there was a Ben and Jerry's next door to Damascus)—and yes: the irony was indeed lost on me. So, these pies are for Oliver and even for me—I mean, I still dig ice cream, don't get me wrong, but these pies are pretty darn tasty, too.

1. Heat the oven to 400°F. Line a baking sheet with parchment paper.

2. Make the filling: Combine all the filling ingredients in a large bowl. Divide the filling into eight portions (about 2 tablespoons [30 g] each). Shape each portion into a log and set them aside.

3. Assemble the hand pies: Divide the pie dough into nine pieces (about 48 g each), and cover with a clean dish towel (the dough is easier to work with when warm). Roll out one piece into a 4½-inch square, picking it up and rotating it as you do so. You shouldn't need to flour your work surface, as the dough isn't very sticky, but you can roll the dough between two pieces of parchment for extra insurance. Brush the square with mayonnaise, leaving a ½-inch bare border around the edges, and place a portion of the filling in the center. Brush the border with egg wash and fold the dough over on the diagonal, creating a triangle. Press the edges together first with your fingertips, and then further seal them with a fork. Repeat with the remaining dough and filling.

4. Transfer the pies to the prepared baking sheet, brush them with egg wash, and sprinkle them with sesame seeds (if using).

5. Bake for 20 to 25 minutes, rotating at the halfway point, until golden on top and bottom. Remove from the oven and let cool for at least 10 minutes before serving warm or at room temperature.

Mushroom Cap Pasties

MAKES 8 PASTIES
ACTIVE TIME: 30 MINUTES
BAKE TIME: 20 TO 25 MINUTES

FILLING

One batch 4-Minute Mushrooms
(page 238), at room
temperature

2 tablespoons finely chopped
fresh parsley

¼ teaspoon garlic powder

½ teaspoon onion powder

¾ teaspoon kosher salt

¼ teaspoon freshly ground
black pepper

⅛ teaspoon cayenne pepper,
or to taste

4 ounces (113 g) full-fat
cream cheese, at cool
room temperature

3 tablespoons finely
grated Parmesan

1 large egg, cold,
lightly beaten

PASTIES

One batch Magic Melted
Butter Pie Dough × 1
(page 233)

Mayonnaise for brushing

The Ultimate Egg Wash
(page 230)

A "pasty" is a traditional English meat pie. But because mushrooms are pretty hearty (and dare I say "meaty") in their own lovely and vegetal way, I thought it might be fun to make a *mushroom* pasty (and, spoiler alert: it is). Moreover, cream cheese–stuffed mushroom caps are, like, my forever faves, and thus these little pastry-filled-pies with cap vibes to boot, are just too good to be true in my book (both literally and figuratively).

1. Heat the oven to 400°F. Line a baking sheet with parchment paper.

2. Season the 4-minute mushrooms with the parsley, garlic and onion powders, salt, black pepper, and cayenne in a medium bowl, using a fork. In another medium bowl, mix together the two cheeses and egg and then fold in the seasoned mushrooms.

3. Divide the pie dough into eight pieces (about 53 g each), and cover with a clean dish towel (the dough is easier to work with when warm). Roll out one piece into a 5-inch circle, picking it up and rotating it as you do so. You shouldn't need to flour your work surface, but you can roll the dough between two pieces of parchment for extra insurance. Brush with mayonnaise, leaving a ½-inch bare border around the edge, and place 2 tablespoons (about 35 g) of the filling in the center, shaping it into a log. Brush the border with egg wash and fold the circle into a half-moon. Press the edges together with your fingertips, and then seal with a fork. Repeat with the remaining dough and filling.

4. Transfer the pasties to the prepared baking sheet and brush them with egg wash.

5. Bake for 20 to 25 minutes, rotating at the halfway point, until they are golden on top and bottom. Let cool to room temperature before serving (my preference) or serve warm.

Chili Crisp Sour Cream Flatbreads
WITH MELTY CHEESE

MAKES 8 FLATBREADS
ACTIVE TIME: 10 MINUTES
REST TIME: 20 TO 30 MINUTES
COOK TIME: 6 MINUTES PER FLATBREAD

2 cups (260 g) all-purpose flour
1½ teaspoons kosher salt
1¼ teaspoons baking powder
1 cup (230 g) full-fat sour cream
Neutral oil for brushing
About 3 tablespoons chili crisp, plus its oil for brushing (see headnote for tips)
1 cup (100 g) shredded cheese (your choice) for sprinkling

VARIATION

For Spicy Calabrian Chili Flat-breads with Mozzarella, sub-stitute olive oil for the neutral oil and Calabrian chili oil (from a jar of Calabrian chile peppers), for the chili crisp oil, substitute ½ teaspoon chopped Calabrian pep-pers per bread for the chili crisp; sprinkle with shredded mozzarella. If the chili oil is crazy hot, brush with olive oil instead.

I love these flatbreads made with tangy, rich sour cream instead of the traditional yogurt. They make for the perfect little snack on their own, but are also wonderful topped with some refried beans and avocado or an egg and additional cheese. The short rest allows the gluten in the dough to relax and ensures the flatbreads will roll out easily without spring-ing back. And pro tip: If your jar of chili crisp doesn't have a few extra tablespoons of oil resting atop the crispy bits, stir 2 to 3 tablespoons of neutral oil into the jar. Let it sit while you assemble and rest the bread. The crisp will resettle to the bottom of the jar, and a layer of freshly infused chili oil will be left floating on top.

1. Have ready a 10- or 12-inch skillet. Line a baking sheet with parchment paper.

2. Whisk together the flour, salt, and baking powder in a large bowl. Fold in the sour cream with a flexible spatula (switching over to your hands once the dough starts to come together) until the sour cream is combined with the flour mixture. Form the dough into a ball, transfer it to a lightly floured work surface, and knead for about a minute, or until smooth. Cover with a clean dish towel or plastic wrap and let rest for 20 to 30 minutes.

3. Pour 2 to 3 tablespoons of chili crisp oil from the top of your jar into a small bowl and set aside for brushing. Warm the skil-let over medium heat and heat the oven to 300°F. Divide the dough into eight pieces (about 60 g each) and re-cover with your dish towel or plastic wrap. With a rolling pin (no need to flour your work surface), roll one piece into a ⅛-inch-thick roundish or oblong shape. To cook, brush one side with neu-tral oil and place, oil side down, in the heated skillet. Cook for 3 minutes, or until puffed and lightly browned. Meanwhile, prepare the next piece of dough by rolling it out and brushing one side with neutral oil.

4. Flip the bread in the pan, brush with the reserved chili crisp oil, drizzle about 1 teaspoon of the oil-soaked crispy bits onto the bread, and sprinkle with 2 tablespoons of cheese. Cook for another 3 minutes, then transfer to the prepared baking sheet and place in the oven to keep warm. Repeat with the remaining pieces of dough, wiping out the skillet periodically to remove burnt chili crisp, if necessary. Serve warm.

Olive Oil and Black Pepper Popovers

MAKES 6 LARGE POPOVERS,
USING A POPOVER PAN, OR
12 SMALLER POPOVERS, USING
A 12-WELL MUFFIN TIN

ACTIVE TIME: 5 MINUTES

BAKE TIME: 30 MINUTES

4 large eggs, at room
temperature

¾ cup (180 g) nonfat milk, at
room temperature or warm

2 tablespoons olive oil,
something deliciously
flavorful that you love

1 cup (130 g) all-purpose flour

¾ teaspoon kosher salt

1¼ teaspoons freshly ground
black pepper

I am literally a popover whisperer, but only after many years of popover making and internet sleuthing (aka researching). So, I've got science to drop. For instance, nonfat milk makes for the crispiest of popovers (but you can substitute whole) AND room temperature ingredients are key for tall popovers (the milk can be warmed in the microwave—no judgment). Resting your batter for 30 to 60 minutes or overnight also results in statuesque popovers, but honestly, resting is just too fussy for me. Feel free to omit the black pepper and serve with salted butter and jam, if you're feeling all breakfast-y.

___

1. Heat the oven to 425°F, position a rack in the lower third, and place a 6-well popover pan or 12-well muffin tin inside.

2. Whisk together the eggs, milk, and oil in a medium bowl until frothy. Add the flour, salt, and pepper and continue to whisk until combined, about 30 seconds. A few little lumps are fine. The batter should be thin and pourable.

3. Carefully remove the hot pan from the oven with pot holder–clad hands and grease the wells with cooking spray. Equally divide the batter among the wells, filling each about half full.

4. Bake for 30 minutes if using a popover pan; bake for 25 minutes if using a muffin tin. Do not open the oven for the entire baking period.

5. Remove from the oven and immediately remove the popovers from the pan or tin, poking each with a wooden skewer to release steam. Serve immediately.

Salami, Brie, and Figgy Mini Pies

MAKES 12 MINI PIES
ACTIVE TIME: 20 MINUTES
BAKE TIME: 15 TO 20 MINUTES

One batch Magic Melted
    Butter Pie Dough × 1
    (page 233)

The Ultimate Egg Wash
    (page 230)

6 ounces (170 g) Brie, cold, cut
    into 12 pieces

¼ cup (80 g) fig jam
    or preserves

¾ cup (84 g) chopped
    thinly sliced salami, ¼ to
    ½-inch pieces

1 tablespoon chopped
    fresh thyme

The combo of creamy Brie, salty salami, and sweet figgy jam makes for perfect little savory mini pies; and said pies, make for the perfect cover girls. Deli salami, thinly sliced, like what you'd layer on a sandwich, is what you want here (not the stuff that comes shaped like a log). Chilling the Brie facilitates cutting it; and although I love the combo of regular salami and fig jam best, a spicier salami with maybe some apricot jam or even honey, drizzled on before and after baking, would work, too. The recipe calls for rolling out the dough into tiny circles with a rolling pin, but I've been known to just pat them out with my hands (I mean, easy-peasy for life, and all that).

1. Heat the oven to 400°F. Grease a 12-well muffin tin with cooking spray.

2. Divide the pie dough into 12 balls (about 36 g each) and cover with a clean dish towel to keep warm (the dough is easier to work with when warm). Roll out one piece into a 3½-inch circle, picking it up and rotating it as you do so. You shouldn't need to flour your work surface, as the dough isn't very sticky, but you can roll the dough between two pieces of parchment for extra insurance. Press the circle into one of the prepared wells, so it adheres to the bottom and sides. The dough will not reach the top of the well—don't worry. Repeat with the remaining pieces of dough. Brush the edges with egg wash (it's nice to do so before you fill the pies).

3. Put about 1 teaspoon of jam in the bottom of each pie, evenly divide the salami between the pies and then the Brie pieces, slicing them in half to fit. Sprinkle the mini pies with the thyme.

4. Bake for 15 to 20 minutes, until the cheese is bubbly and browned. Remove from the oven and let rest for about 5 minutes, or until you can safely touch the pan without burning yourself. Gently pull the warm pies from the tin, running a small offset spatula or butter knife around the edges if they resist. Serve warm or at room temperature.

CHAPTER 4

Brunchables, Lunchables, and Even Dinnerables

Still can't quite believe that I (little old sweet-loving me) wrote a cookbook with a chapter of baked goods that you can eat for dinner. I mean, crazy, no?! But I did, and I'm pretty sure that we're all the luckier—and soon to be wonderfully satiated—for it. Items in this chapter tend to bake a tad longer than some of the salty, cheesy, herby, crispy treats elsewhere in the book, but nothing longer than an hour (if that). Every recipe in the chapter works for every meal of the day—as long as you're okay eating spaghetti for brunch (page 123), which for the record, I am. And just a little shout-out to my three savory galettes with easy Magic Melted Butter Pie Dough (pages 124, 126, and 129), as the dough is so easy, the fillings so simple and the finished product so pretty, so flavorful, and so fun.

Pro Tips, Fun Facts, and Storing/Reheating Instructions

- Please do not get anxious if the edges of your melted butter pie dough crack as you fold them over your galette filling—this dough is an absolute love to work with, and some finger pinching is all you need to do to seal those cracks right back up—**and galettes are supposed to be RUSTIC**, anyway.

- My easy-peasy **method for steaming spinach** is tucked away in the recipe for Spinach Artichoke "Dip" Strata (page 130), and all I can say is: she's a keeper.

- You actually **cook the bacon in the same pan that you bake the "Yorkie" pudding in** (as we dig a one-pan meal over here in Snackable Bakes Land) and the bacon may take a tad longer to get crispy than it does

for you to assemble the rest of the "Yorkie" ingredients—but relax: patience is a virtue (which I have none of, FYI) and the batter benefits from a rest, anyway.

TO STORE: Brunchables, etc. are best eaten the day they are made, fresh from the oven and still warm (or at room temperature, if preferred), but will last up to 3 days, tightly wrapped, in the refrigerator or in the freezer for up to a month. The exceptions: The "Yorkie" lasts only 1 night in the refrigerator; and the Tomato Cobbler, only two—and neither should be frozen. The granola, on the other hand, will last, in an airtight container, on the counter for about a month.

TO REHEAT: Reheat room-temperature brunchables, etc. in a 300°F oven on a parchment-lined baking sheet, or in the dish in which they were baked, until warm, about 10 minutes; do just 5 minutes, for the "Yorkie."

Savory Granola

WITH PECANS, PEPITAS, AND COCONUT

MAKES ABOUT 8 CUPS
ACTIVE TIME: 5 MINUTES
BAKE TIME: 45 MINUTES

¼ cup (59 g) coconut oil, melted

3 tablespoons pure maple syrup

2½ tablespoons soy sauce

2 large egg whites

2 teaspoons kosher salt

½ teaspoon cayenne pepper

¾ teaspoon red pepper flakes

2 cups (200 g) quick one-minute oats

1½ cups (150 g) pecans, chopped roughly

1 cup (140 g) raw pumpkin seeds (aka pepitas)

1½ cups (67 g) unsweetened coconut flakes

Flaky sea salt for sprinkling

It took me a moment to jump on board with savory granola, I won't lie, but I've now jumped and couldn't be happier. It is perfect sprinkled on a salad or over yogurt, as well as spooned from a bowl with milk or eaten out of hand. The inclusion of the two egg whites here is not cool, I know, but if you are proclump, you'll need them. Because savory granola has very little sugar (just a bit of maple syrup), the whites are exclusively responsible for the telltale clumping-together of ingredients that enthusiastically draws us all to the granola party in the first place. Moreover, you can substitute them for the whole egg in the Ultimate Egg-Wash (page 230).

1. Heat the oven to 350°F. Line a baking sheet with parchment paper.

2. Whisk together the oil, maple syrup, soy sauce, egg whites, salt, cayenne, and red pepper flakes in a large bowl. Mix in the oats, pecans, pumpkin seeds, and coconut with your hands or a flexible spatula, until all are coated with the oil mixture.

3. Evenly spread the granola on the prepared baking sheet and bake for about 45 minutes, rotating the pan and lowering the oven temperature to 325°F at the halfway point. For an extra-clumpy granola, resist the urge to stir while it bakes. The granola is ready when it has darkened in color and is deliciously fragrant.

4. Remove from the oven and immediately sprinkle with the flaky salt. Let sit until the granola hardens and cools before serving.

Eggy Cheesy Open-Face Tarts

MAKES 4 TARTS

ACTIVE TIME: 15 MINUTES

BAKE TIME: 20 TO 22 MINUTES

One batch Magic Melted
  Butter Pie Dough × 1
  (page 233)

The Ultimate Egg Wash
  (page 230)

Mayonnaise for brushing

4 slices American cheese, or
  your favorite

4 large eggs

Kosher salt for sprinkling

Freshly ground black pepper
  for sprinkling

Hot sauce, scallions, herbs,
  salsa, for serving (optional)

Oh my gosh—there is something about eating an egg and cheese sandwich, open-face on buttery pastry, that just checks all the "new favorite thing" boxes. Topping the pastry with the egg and cheese midway through baking makes for a runny yolk—but if runny is not how you roll, fully assemble the tart before placing it in the oven and all your hard-set yolk dreams will come true. For a darker crust, parbake for closer to 15 minutes, rather than 10.

1. Heat the oven to 400°F. Line a baking sheet with parchment paper.

2. Divide the pie dough into four pieces (about 106 g each), and cover with a clean dish towel to keep warm (the dough is easier to work with when warm). Roll out one piece into a 6-by-8-inch rectangle, picking it up and rotating it as you do so. You shouldn't need to flour your work surface, as the dough isn't very sticky, but you can roll the dough between two pieces of parchment for extra insurance. Roll up the pastry on each side, to create a raised border, just until the rectangle measures 4 by 5 inches. Crimp the border with your fingertips, if you so desire, to give it a little extra height, as this border will prevent the egg white from escaping the tart.

3. Transfer the pastry shell to the prepared baking sheet, brush the raised border with egg wash, and dock the bottom several times with a fork. Repeat with the remaining three pieces of dough.

4. Bake the pastry shells for 10 to 15 minutes. Remove from the oven, gently press down the bottoms, if they've puffed, brush with mayonnaise, and top each with a slice of cheese. Crack an egg over the cheese, sprinkle with salt and pepper, and carefully return the sheet of tarts back to the oven to bake for 10 to 12 more minutes, or until the whites have just set. Serve immediately with your favorite toppings.

5. Egg tarts should be eaten warm from the oven.

Jack's Tomato Cobbler
WITH PARMESAN CREAM BISCUITS

MAKES ONE 8-INCH COBBLER
ACTIVE TIME: 15 MINUTES
BAKE TIME: 45 TO 50 MINUTES

FILLING
2 tablespoons cornstarch

3 tablespoons finely grated
   Parmesan, plus more
   for sprinkling

2 teaspoons granulated sugar

¾ teaspoon kosher salt

½ teaspoon freshly ground
   black pepper

½ teaspoon dried thyme

¼ teaspoon red pepper flakes

¼ teaspoon garlic powder

2 pounds (907 g) cherry
   tomatoes, sliced in half

3 tablespoons olive oil

One batch Best-Ever Cream
   Biscuit Dough with
   Parmesan (page 234)

The Ultimate Egg Wash
   (page 230)

Originally, this (out-of-this-world) tomato cobbler was going to be a *chicken* cobbler for my younger son, Jack, as he is a chicken potpie lover from way back. But prepping the chicken, gravy, veggies, etc. for Jack's fave did not seem like the easy-peasiest of exercises, and so I quickly changed direction and we ended up here: with juicy, soft, seasoned tomatoes crowned with fluffy Parm biscuits that soak up the jammy sauce like nobody's business. I don't think you're going to miss the chicken (but Jack def will, as he is not too crazy about tomatoes . . . oops).

1. Heat the oven to 350°F. Grease an 8-inch square baking pan with cooking spray or olive oil and have ready a baking sheet.

2. Make the filling: Whisk together the cornstarch, Parmesan, sugar, salt, black pepper, thyme, red pepper flakes, and garlic powder in a large bowl. Add the tomatoes, drizzle with the oil, and toss to coat with your hands or a flexible spatula. Transfer the tomatoes to the prepared baking pan.

3. Scoop the dough into nine biscuits, using a ¼-cup portion scoop, if you have one, or a measuring cup, and evenly place them over the tomatoes. Brush with egg wash and sprinkle with extra Parmesan.

4. Place the cobbler pan on the baking sheet and bake for 45 to 50 minutes, rotating at the halfway point, until the biscuits are nicely browned and the tomatoes are bubbling up between them. Remove from the oven, let cool for about 10 minutes, and serve warm.

Garlicky Creamed Greens Pie

MAKES ONE 9-INCH PIE
ACTIVE TIME: 25 MINUTES
BAKE TIME: 35 TO 40 MINUTES

GREENS
¼ cup (50 g) olive oil

3 tablespoons minced garlic

2 pounds (907 g) hearty greens, such as spinach, dinosaur kale, and Swiss chard (about 3 bunches), stems removed, leaves sliced into ribbons and chopped roughly

1 teaspoon kosher salt

½ teaspoon freshly ground black pepper

½ teaspoon garlic powder

2 tablespoons cornstarch

1¼ cups (300 g) heavy cream

4 ounces (113 g) full-fat cream cheese

½ teaspoon freshly grated nutmeg

PIE
One batch Magic Melted Butter Pie Dough—Single Crust (page 233)

2 tablespoons panko bread crumbs

My birthday tradition is a steak dinner at Peter Luger's in Brooklyn, and although I adore the steak (and the copious amounts of whipped cream [aka schlag] served with every dessert), I'm really all about the creamed spinach. Something about the combo of cream and spinach just works for me in the most delicious of ways. This pie is a love letter to that dish, but with kale and Swiss chard thrown in for good measure. Yes, cleaning, stemming, and cutting greens is time-consuming, as is mincing 3 tablespoons of garlic . . . so, if you can find pre-washed greens in bags and jarred minced garlic, I encourage you to purchase and use both with abandon.

———

1. Heat the oven to 400°F. Have ready a 9-inch pie plate.

2. Make the greens: Heat the oil in a large pot over medium to medium-high heat and add the garlic. Cook until fragrant, about 1 minute. Add the greens, salt, pepper, and garlic powder to the pot and cook, covered, until wilted, stirring frequently with a flexible spatula, 8 to 10 minutes. Whisk the cornstarch into the heavy cream in a small bowl, pour the mixture over the greens, and bring to a boil, about 1 minute. Remove from the heat and stir in the cream cheese until it fully melts. Stir in the nutmeg and let cool (preferably in the refrigerator) while you make the pie dough.

3. Using your fingers, evenly press the pie dough onto the bottom and up the sides of the pie plate, crimping the edge with a fork, if you so desire. Sprinkle the bottom with the bread crumbs.

4. Transfer the filling to the crust and bake for 35 to 40 minutes, until the center of the filling is set and the crust is browned. Remove from the oven and let cool on a wire rack until just warm or at room temperature, and serve.

Baked Spaghetti "Pie"

WITH CHEESY MARINARA

MAKES ONE 8-INCH ROUND
SPAGHETTI "PIE"
ACTIVE TIME: 20 MINUTES
BAKE TIME: 30 MINUTES

Olive oil for brushing the pan

¾ cup plus 2 tablespoons (88 g)
finely grated Parmesan,
divided, plus more
for serving

2 large eggs

1½ cups (382 g) store-bought
or homemade marinara
sauce, plus more
for serving

¾ teaspoon kosher salt,
or to taste

½ teaspoon freshly ground
black pepper

½ to ¾ teaspoon garlic powder

½ to ¾ teaspoon dried oregano

1¼ cups (125 g) shredded
low-moisture whole-milk
mozzarella, divided, plus
more for sprinkling

⅓ cup (76 g) ricotta

¾ pound (340 g) spaghetti,
cooked until al dente

I am obsessed with this spaghetti pie due to the magic that is baking it in a cake pan. My fave store-bought marinara sauce is Rao's brand, and if you want to make your own, Marcella Hazan has a fabulous one with only three ingredients—and depending on how flavorful your chosen sauce is, be it purchased or homemade, you can go up or down with the garlic and onion powders. Oh, and a pro tip: Wrap the spaghetti in a clean dish towel (which will prevent you from spraying your kitchen with tiny broken noodles. You're welcome.) and break the spaghetti into thirds before boiling it, as it'll cook faster (in only 5 minutes!) and the pie will be easier to slice and eat.

1. Heat the oven to 350°F. Brush an 8-inch round cake pan with olive oil and line the bottom with parchment paper. Brush the parchment with additional oil and sprinkle the bottom and sides of the pan with ¼ cup (25 g) of the Parmesan to coat.

2. Lightly whisk the eggs in a large bowl. Whisk in the marinara, salt, pepper, garlic powder, oregano, ½ cup (50 g) of the Parmesan, ¾ cup (75 g) of the mozzarella, and the ricotta. Fold in the cooked spaghetti with a flexible spatula and transfer the mixture to the prepared cake pan, pressing down with your spatula to compress it. Sprinkle the remaining 2 tablespoons of Parmesan over the top.

3. Bake for about 15 minutes. Carefully remove the cake pan from the oven, sprinkle the "pie" with the remaining ½ cup (50g) of mozzarella, and return the pan to the oven to bake for about 15 minutes more, or until the cheese is nicely melted. If you want your cheese bronzed and slightly crispy, place the pie under the broiler briefly, keeping a watchful eye, about 2 minutes or so.

4. Remove from the oven and let cool for 10 minutes before running a knife around the edge of the pan and inverting the "pie" onto a serving plate (you may need to give the bottom of the cake pan a few firm taps to help it release). Let it rest for 5 to 10 more minutes, then serve the "pie" in wedges, passing extra Parmesan and sauce, if desired, at the table.

Tomato Za'atar Galette
WITH ONION AND CHEESE

My Magic Melted Butter Pie Dough (page 233) makes for the absolute best, crispy, yet buttery-crusted galettes and is sturdy enough to handle ingredients like fresh tomatoes. Moreover, the nutty, sharp Parmesan in the dough is wonderful with said tomatoes and the slivers of red onions and creamy, milky mozzarella. If you can't find za'atar, substitute Italian seasoning or oregano, or make your own (page 58)!

MAKES ONE 9-INCH GALETTE
ACTIVE TIME: 15 MINUTES
BAKE TIME: 40 TO 50 MINUTES

1¼ pounds (569 g) colorful heirloom tomatoes, or regular ones, sliced ¼ inch thick

2 teaspoons kosher salt, divided

One batch Magic Melted Butter Pie Dough × 1 with Parmesan (page 233)

1½ teaspoons za'atar spice blend, divided

1 teaspoon garlic powder

¼ teaspoon red pepper flakes, or to taste

1¼ cups (125 g) shredded low-moisture whole-milk mozzarella

¼ cup (35 g) thinly sliced red onion

Freshly ground black pepper for sprinkling

The Ultimate Egg Wash (page 230)

Olive oil for drizzling

Flaky sea salt for sprinkling

1. Heat the oven to 400°F. Have ready a baking sheet.

2. Set a colander over a plate or in the sink, and layer the tomato slices inside, sprinkling them with 1 teaspoon of salt as you do so. Give the colander an occasional gentle shake as you make the crust, to release excess liquid from the tomatoes.

3. Shape the Parmesan pie dough into a flat disk and roll it out between two pieces of parchment paper until it is about ¼ inch thick and round(ish) in shape. Place the dough, still between the sheets of paper, on the baking sheet and peel off the top sheet.

4. Pat the drained tomatoes with a paper towel, transfer to the bowl you used to make the dough, and sprinkle with the remaining teaspoon of salt, ½ teaspoon of the za'atar, garlic powder, and red pepper flakes. Gently stir with a flexible spatula. Sprinkle the cheese over the bottom of the dough, leaving a 2-inch bare border around the edge. Cover the cheese with the tomatoes, scatter the onion slices on top, and sprinkle with the remaining teaspoon of za'atar and black pepper. Fold up the edges of the dough, and if cracks form, press them back together with your fingers. Squeeze the dough folds together and brush with egg wash. Drizzle the tomatoes with olive oil.

5. Bake the galette for 40 to 50 minutes, until the tomatoes collapse and the crust browns. Remove from the oven and sprinkle with flaky salt. Let cool for 10 minutes before slicing with a pizza cutter or sharp chef's knife.

Pepperoni "Pizza" Galette
WITH RICOTTA

MAKES ONE 9-INCH GALETTE
ACTIVE TIME: 15 MINUTES
BAKE TIME: 30 TO 35 MINUTES

1 cup (227 g) ricotta
½ teaspoon kosher salt
½ teaspoon freshly ground black pepper
½ teaspoon dried oregano
¼ teaspoon garlic powder
¼ teaspoon onion powder
¼ teaspoon red pepper flakes, or to taste
One batch Magic Melted Butter Pie Dough × 1 with Parmesan (page 233)
⅓ cup (85 g) store-bought or homemade marinara sauce
¼ cup plus 2 tablespoons (37 g) finely grated Parmesan
12 thin slices pepperoni
The Ultimate Egg Wash (page 230)
Olive oil for drizzling

Pepperoni pizza is kind of a family fave and, fun fact: you can buy perfectly pizza-size pepperoni slices, prepackaged, at the grocery store (yay!). Traditionally a pepperoni pie is made with mozzarella, but in my galette version, I like to use soft, smooth ricotta, as it becomes so wonderfully flavorful and fragrant when combined with the spices herein. If you're buying store-bought marinara sauce for this pie ("pizza" pie, that is), see my Baked Spaghetti "Pie" (page 123) for my fave. And consider sprinkling the pie before serving with a few small leaves of fresh basil or flat-leaf parsley, for a little color *and* if you know what's good for you (which I know you do).

1. Heat the oven to 400°F. Have ready a baking sheet.

2. Combine the ricotta, salt, black pepper, oregano, garlic and onion powders, and red pepper flakes in a small bowl, using a fork.

3. Place the Parmesan pie dough on a long sheet of parchment paper and shape it into a flat disk in the center of the sheet. Place another sheet of parchment paper on top and roll out the dough until it is about ¼ inch thick and round(ish) in shape. Place the dough, still between the sheets of paper, on the baking sheet and peel off the top sheet.

4. Spread the marinara over the dough, leaving about a 2-inch bare border around the edge, and sprinkle with the Parmesan. Dollop the seasoned ricotta mixture over the tomato sauce. Evenly arrange the pepperoni over the ricotta. Gently fold up the edges of the dough, and if cracks form, just press them back together with your fingers. Decoratively squeeze the dough folds together and brush with egg wash. Drizzle the cheese and pepperoni with a little olive oil.

5. Bake the galette for 30 to 35 minutes, rotating at the halfway point, until the pepperoni is crispy and the crust is browned. Remove from the oven and let cool briefly before slicing with a pizza cutter, if you have one, or chef's knife.

Basil Peach Mascarpone Galette

MAKES ONE 9-INCH GALETTE
ACTIVE TIME: 15 MINUTES
BAKE TIME: 30 TO 40 MINUTES

1 cup (227 g) mascarpone
½ teaspoon kosher salt
½ teaspoon dried basil
¼ teaspoon garlic powder
¼ teaspoon red pepper flakes, or to taste
¼ teaspoon freshly ground black pepper, plus more for sprinkling
1 teaspoon freshly squeezed lemon juice, or a mild vinegar, such as white wine
⅓ cup (33 g) shredded low-moisture whole-milk mozzarella
¾ pound (340 g) pitted and sliced peaches, about ¼ inch thick
One batch Magic Melted Butter Pie Dough × 1 with Basil (page 233)
The Ultimate Egg Wash (page 230)
Olive oil for drizzling
Flaky sea salt for sprinkling
Fresh basil leaves for garnish

This cutie's a beauty, peeps (and, yes, I'm a poet and didn't even know it). Serve with slices of prosciutto, for the meat-lovers in your life, and cool to almost room temperature before serving as this gives the galette a little time to firm up and reabsorb the pooled peach juice. Peach and mascarpone (a richer relative of cream cheese) work deliciously here, especially with the fresh basil sprinkled on postbake, which contributes both slightly sweet and savory vibes to an already sweet yet savory situation.

1. Heat the oven to 400°F. Have ready a baking sheet.

2. Combine the mascarpone, salt, basil, garlic powder, red pepper flakes, black pepper, and lemon juice in a small bowl, using a fork.

3. Place the basil pie dough on a long sheet of parchment paper and shape it into a flat disk in the center of the sheet. Place another sheet of parchment paper on top and roll out the dough until it is about ¼ inch thick and round(ish) in shape. Place the dough, still between the sheets of paper, on the baking sheet and peel off the top sheet.

4. Spread the mascarpone mixture over the dough, leaving about a 2-inch bare border around the edge, and sprinkle with the mozzarella. Arrange the peaches over the cheeses, overlapping them as necessary. Gently fold up the edges of the dough, and if cracks form, just press them back together with your fingers. Decoratively squeeze the dough folds together and brush with egg wash. Drizzle the peaches with olive oil and sprinkle with a few grinds of black pepper.

5. Bake the galette for 30 to 40 minutes, rotating at the halfway point, until the peaches collapse and bubble and the crust browns. Remove from the oven, sprinkle with flaky sea salt, and garnish with fresh basil leaves (snipped, torn or, if small, left whole). Let the galette cool until just warm before slicing it with a pizza cutter or chef's knife.

Spinach Artichoke "Dip" Strata

MAKES ONE 8-INCH SQUARE
STRATA

ACTIVE TIME: 15 MINUTES

BAKE TIME: ABOUT 35 MINUTES

½ pound (227 g) baby spinach

½ teaspoon red pepper flakes,
or to taste

1 teaspoon kosher salt

½ teaspoon freshly ground
black pepper

One 14-ounce can (397 g)
drained artichoke hearts,
chopped roughly

8 ounces (227 g) full-fat cream
cheese, cut into 16 pieces

1 cup (100 g) shredded low-
moisture whole-milk
mozzarella

¼ cup (25 g) finely grated
Parmesan cheese

8 ounces (227 g) stale
baguette, torn into
bite-size pieces

6 large eggs

2 cups (480 g) whole milk

¼ teaspoon cayenne pepper

½ teaspoon onion powder

A strata is similar, but more eggy than a bread pudding, though they're def related (perhaps first cousins once removed?). The spinach, artichokes and cream cheese "pockets" here are intended to give you all sorts of dip vibes, and the toasty bits on top postbake are almost like the crackers you'd use to scoop up said dip, as Steph observed, when she tested it. Use a day-old baguette, if you have one, or tear up a fresh one the night before and leave it on the counter overnight to go stale. In a same-day pinch, tearing fresh bread and toasting it on a baking sheet for 15 to 20 minutes at 300°F does the trick, too.

1. Heat the oven to 350°F. Grease an 8-inch square baking pan with cooking spray.

2. Place the spinach in a microwave-safe bowl with a splash of water, cover, and microwave on HIGH, in 45-second bursts, until wilted, about 2 minutes. Squeeze the water from the spinach, dry the bowl, and place the spinach back in it. Separate the spinach a bit with your fingers if it's in a large mass.

3. Sprinkle the red pepper flakes, salt, and black pepper evenly over the spinach, and then stir in the artichokes, cream cheese, mozzarella, and Parmesan with a flexible spatula (or toss with your hands), making sure the spices are evenly distributed. Stir in the bread and transfer to the prepared baking pan.

4. Whisk the eggs in the now-empty bowl—no need to clean it first—and then thoroughly whisk in the milk, cayenne, and onion powder. Pour the custard evenly over the mixture in the baking pan, making sure to soak the top pieces of bread (you can press to submerge them, if necessary). The pan will be very full.

5. Bake for about 35 minutes, rotating at the halfway point, until the strata is lightly browned and slightly puffed, and has an internal temperature of around 170°F. Remove from the oven and let cool for about 10 minutes. Cut into slices and serve warm.

Mushroom and Mozzarella Skillet Bread Pudding

MAKES ONE 10-INCH ROUND
BREAD PUDDING
ACTIVE TIME: 15 MINUTES
BAKE TIME: 30 TO 35 MINUTES

One batch 4-Minute Mush-
 rooms (page 238), at room
 temperature
½ teaspoon kosher salt
½ teaspoon freshly ground
 black pepper
1 teaspoon dried thyme
1½ cups (150 g) shredded
 low-moisture whole-milk
 mozzarella, plus more
 for sprinkling
8 ounces (227 g) stale brioche
 or challah, cut into
 ¾-inch cubes
4 large eggs
2 cups (480 g) heavy cream
½ cup (120 g) chicken or
 veggie stock

I am a huge mushroom fan and also a mozzarella lover from way back (in fact, it's my favorite cheese). So, to me (and hopefully to you, too), this savory bread pudding is not only comfort in a skillet any time of the day, what with its soft, breadlike yet custardy interior and toasty top bits, but also a delicious mash-up of two fab ingredients. I call for heavy cream here because I am extra, but use half-and-half if you are feeling extra-ish, or whole milk if extra is not your jam. You can use the mushroom cooking liquid for part of the stock for even more mushroom flavor. Check out the headnote for the Spinach Artichoke "Dip" Strata (page 130) for the magic that is turning fresh bread into stale.

1. Heat the oven to 375°F. Grease a 10-inch cast-iron or heat-proof skillet with cooking spray.

2. Season the 4-minute mushrooms in a large bowl with the salt, pepper, and thyme, using a fork. Add the mozzarella and bread and mix to combine with a flexible spatula or your hands. Transfer the mixture to the prepared skillet. Whisk together the eggs, cream, and stock in a 4-cup measuring cup, if you have one, or a large bowl. Pour evenly over the bread mixture, making sure to soak the top pieces (you can press to submerge them, if necessary). Sprinkle the top with a little extra mozzarella.

3. Bake for 30 to 35 minutes, rotating at the halfway point, until the bread pudding is lightly browned and slightly puffed, and has an internal temperature of around 170°F. Remove from the oven and let cool for about 10 minutes. Cut into slices and serve warm.

VARIATION

For Sausage Pizza Skillet Bread Pudding, substitute 1½ cups (170 g) of cooked and crumbled sweet Italian sausage meat (from 8 ounces [227 g] of raw bulk sausage) for the 4-minute mush-rooms, and ¾ teaspoon of dried oregano for the dried thyme. Add ½ cup (97 g) jarred chopped roasted red bell peppers along with the mozzarella and bread.

Cheesy, Peppery Zuke Quiche
WITH A SALTINE CRUST

MAKES ONE 9-INCH QUICHE
ACTIVE TIME: 20 MINUTES
INACTIVE TIME: 15 MINUTES TO
CHILL THE CRUST PREBAKE,
PLUS ABOUT 20 MINUTES TO
COOL IT POSTBAKE
BAKE TIME: 45 TO 50 MINUTES,
DIVIDED

SALTINE CRUST
1½ sleeves (192 g) saltines or
   soda crackers
¾ cup (169 g) unsalted butter,
   melted and cooled slightly

FILLING
1¼ cups (160 g) grated zucchini
   (about 1 medium unpeeled
   zucchini)
3 large eggs
½ cup (120 g) heavy cream
½ cup (113 g) cottage cheese,
   2% fat or higher
¾ teaspoon kosher salt
½ teaspoon freshly ground
   black pepper
¼ teaspoon cayenne pepper
½ teaspoon red pepper flakes
1¼ cups (125 g) shredded melty
   cheese, your fave

VARIATION

For Cheesy, Peppery Broccoli
Quiche, replace the zucchini
with 4 ounces (113 g) raw broccoli, chopped small (1½ cups).

This recipe took a billion tests to get right, from melted butter pie dough crusts to Ritz cracker crumb crusts and, finally, to the perfect crust (aka one made with saltines). I like the combo of zucchini and cheese here, as the zuke almost melts into the custard and results in a filling that is creaminess personified. Cottage cheese is having a moment—hence her inclusion here—AND she keeps the custard from being too loose and softening the crust. The crust is crumbly and tastes very saltine-y in the best way, but it is not supercrispy. Choose a softish cheese that melts nicely, such as Monterey Jack, Gouda, or Havarti.

1. Heat the oven to 350°F. Have ready a 9-inch pie plate.

2. Make the crust: Process the saltines in a food processor until finely ground. Pour in the melted butter and process until the mixture holds together when squeezed. Alternatively, place the saltines in a resealable plastic bag, seal carefully, cover with a tea towel, and smash with a rolling pin. Transfer the crumbs to a medium bowl, add the melted butter and stir to combine. Firmly press the mixture onto the bottom and up the sides of the pie plate and freeze for 15 minutes.

3. Bake the crust for about 15 minutes, or until fragrant and lightly browned. Remove from the oven and let come to room temperature before adding the filling (stick the pie plate in the freezer for 15 minutes to speed this up). If the crust puffs up while it bakes or the sides slump a little, use the bottom of a measuring cup or the back of a spoon to press down the bottom of the crust and/or to gently straighten the sides. Increase the oven temperature to 375°F.

4. Make the filling: Squeeze the grated zucchini in a clean dish towel or paper towels to release its liquid. Whisk the eggs, cream, cottage cheese, salt, black pepper, cayenne, and red pepper flakes in a 2-cup measuring cup, if you have one, or a medium bowl. Sprinkle half of the shredded cheese over the bottom of the crust, followed by the zucchini and then the other half of the shredded cheese, then evenly pour the custard over all.

5. Bake for 30 to 35 minutes, until the filling is golden and the center is just set. Remove from the oven and let cool on a wire rack until room temperature or just slightly warm.

Deep-Dish(ish) Cacio e Pepe Quiche

MAKES ONE 8-INCH QUICHE
ACTIVE TIME: 20 MINUTES
BAKE TIME: 55 MINUTES, DIVIDED

HOT WATER PASTRY DOUGH

2 cups (260 g) all-purpose flour
¾ teaspoon kosher salt
1 teaspoon granulated sugar
½ teaspoon baking powder
¼ cup (56 g) unsalted butter
½ cup (116 g) water

FILLING

1 cup (100 g) finely grated Pecorino Romano or Parmesan
1 tablespoon freshly ground black pepper, not too coarse
The Ultimate Egg Wash (page 230)
4 large eggs
1¼ cups (300 g) half-and-half
½ teaspoon kosher salt

This cheese (*cacio*) and pepper (*pepe*) quiche is deep-dish(ish) due to the fact it is baked in an 8-inch cake pan. I adore the straight sides, which apparently allow the custard to cook more evenly (who knew?). The hot water pie dough, though not crazy flavorful, is superstable and strong, and thus allows for the most elegant of freestanding quiches. Moreover, the custard here is pungent, and thus the slightly—dare I say—neutral-flavored dough is its perfect match. Consider this a great blank canvas quiche—throw in some ham, bacon, scallions, or peppers, if you're feeling frisky.

1. Heat the oven to 450°F. Grease an 8-inch round cake pan with 2-inch sides with cooking spray.

2. Make the hot water pastry dough: Whisk together the flour, salt, sugar, and baking powder in a large bowl. Combine the butter and water in a small saucepan on the stovetop and bring to a boil over high heat. Pour the hot mixture over the flour mixture and stir with a fork until combined. Working quickly, knead the dough a few times in the bowl, using your hands, until it holds together when squeezed and there is no more loose flour—you don't actually want it to come together in a single mass, as warm crumbs are easier to press into the pan. Transfer said crumbs to the prepared pan and, using your fingers, evenly press them onto the bottom of the pan and straight up the sides, leaving just a scant ¼-inch space between the top of the crust and the rim of the cake pan.

3. Crumple up a sheet or parchment paper and snugly tuck it into the pan, fill with pie weights (I use uncooked rice), and bake for 15 minutes. Carefully remove the weights and paper (the sides may have slumped a little; don't worry), dock the bottom with a fork, and bake for another 5 minutes, or until the pastry looks dry. Remove from the oven and let cool while you make the filling. Lower the oven temperature to 375°F.

4. Make the filling: Whisk the pecorino and pepper together in a small bowl and sprinkle it over the bottom of the crust. Brush

the edge of the crust with egg wash. Whisk together the eggs, half-and-half, and salt in a large bowl. Carefully pour the custard into the crust and bake for about 35 minutes, or until the filling is golden and the center just set.

5. Remove from the oven and let cool on a wire rack until room temperature. The crust is quite sturdy and will allow you to remove the quiche from the pan once the filling is set.

Herby Swiss Dutch Baby

MAKES ONE 12-INCH DUTCH BABY
ACTIVE TIME: 10 MINUTES
BAKE TIME: ABOUT 20 MINUTES

4 large eggs, at room temperature

¾ cup (180 g) nonfat or 2% milk, at room temperature (or whole milk, in a pinch)

1 cup (130 g) all-purpose flour

1 teaspoon kosher salt

½ teaspoon freshly ground black pepper

3 tablespoons finely chopped mixed soft fresh herbs, such as chives, parsley, and basil, divided

3 tablespoons unsalted butter

½ cup (38 g) finely grated Swiss cheese, or your fave, plus 2 tablespoons or more for sprinkling postbake

Flaky sea salt for sprinkling (optional)

So, I made this baby quite a few times when testing it, in an effort to create one that was extremely cheesy but also very tall and dramatic postbake. Sometimes cheese can weigh down the batter and prevent the baby's rise. However, once I grated the cheese finely and added it not to, but *on* the batter, I had cracked the code. A little extra cheese postbake is never a bad thing, so add more than the 2 tablespoons called for if you're feeling extra cheesy (which I always am, BTW). Chopping herbs is like—literally—the opposite of fun, I get it: but they're so pretty and tasty here (and always) that I'm hoping you won't hold it against me.

1. Heat the oven to 425°F and place a 12-inch ovenproof skillet inside.

2. Whisk together the eggs and milk in a large bowl until frothy. Add the flour, salt, and pepper and continue to whisk until combined, about 30 seconds. A few little lumps are fine. Whisk in 2 tablespoons of the herbs.

3. Carefully remove the hot pan from the oven with pot holder–clad hands, add the butter, and swirl it around to melt and coat. Whisk the batter once more, pour it into the pan, and sprinkle with ½ cup (38 g) of the cheese.

4. Bake for about 20 minutes, until the baby is lightly browned and has climbed up the sides of the pan. Remove from the oven and immediately sprinkle with the remaining 2 tablespoons of cheese, or more if desired, the remaining tablespoon of herbs, and the flaky salt (if using). Serve immediately.

Bacon Cheddar "Yorkie" Pudding

MAKES ONE 9-BY-13-INCH
YORKIE
PREP TIME: 5 MINUTES
COOK TIME: 18 TO 22 MINUTES

3 ounces (85 g) uncooked
  bacon

4 large eggs, at room
  temperature

¾ cup (180 g) nonfat or 2% milk,
  at room temperature or
  warm (or whole milk, in a
  pinch)

1 cup (130 g) all-purpose flour

¾ teaspoon kosher salt

½ teaspoon freshly ground
  black pepper

⅓ cup (25 g) finely grated
  extra-sharp Cheddar,
  plus 3 tablespoons for
  sprinkling postbake

VARIATION

For a vegetarian Yorkie, omit
the bacon. Place the empty
baking pan in the oven while
it heats and add 2 table-
spoons of unsalted butter,
cubed into the hot pan right
before adding the batter (it
will melt almost instantly).
Swirl the pan to evenly cover
its bottom in butter.

I frequently get reprimanded whenever I post a photo of, or recipe for, popovers, with peeps nicely (and not so nicely) explaining to me that what I have in fact made is called York-shire pudding, *not* "popovers." And as far as I can tell, they are—for all intents and purposes—correct. Save for the fact that Yorkshire pudding is made with beef drippings and is typically served with roast beef, popover batter and Yorkie batter are indeed identical. So, for all my Yorkshire pudding fans in the house, this is for you. Serve it for brekkie with eggs or for dinner with meat or chicken. Check out the popover recipe on page 107 for a few of my popover/Yorkie tips and tricks.

1. Heat the oven to 425°F. Place the bacon slices in a single layer in a 9-by-13-inch baking pan and place the pan in the oven while it heats. It should take 20 to 25 minutes for the bacon to get evenly brown, crispy, and easy to crumble.

2. Whisk together the eggs and milk in a medium bowl until frothy. Whisk in the flour, salt, and pepper. A few tiny lumps are fine. Finally, whisk in the ⅓ cup (25 g) of cheese.

3. Check on the bacon at this point to see if it's browned and crispy. If not, cook it for a few more minutes—the batter actually benefits from a rest, so don't worry about waiting. When the bacon is done, remove it from the oven with pot holder–clad hands and, using a slotted spoon or tongs, transfer the bacon to a plate. Scrape the bottom of the pan if any bacon stuck, and swirl the fat so it uniformly coats the pan. Whisk the batter a final time and pour it into the pan, tilting the pan to help the batter reach the corners.

4. Bake for 18 to 22 minutes, until the sides have puffed up and browned and the bottom looks dry, and a little wrinkly. Do not open the oven for at least the first half of the baking time, as it can cause the pudding to deflate. Remove from the oven and sprinkle with the extra 3 tablespoons of cheese. Crumble the cooked bacon over the top. Use a large metal spatula to dislodge the bottom of the Yorkie from the pan if there is any sticking. Serve immediately.

Easy "Western" Spoonbread

MAKES ONE 8-INCH SQUARE
SPOONBREAD
ACTIVE TIME: 10 MINUTES
BAKE TIME: ABOUT 35 MINUTES

½ cup (113 g) unsalted butter,
    melted and cooled slightly

1 cup (240 g) heavy cream or
    whole milk

1 cup (230 g) full-fat sour cream

2 large eggs

2 teaspoons baking powder

¼ teaspoon baking soda

1 tablespoon granulated sugar

1 teaspoon kosher salt

½ teaspoon freshly ground
    black pepper

¾ cup (109 g) medium-grind
    cornmeal

¾ cup (97 g) all-purpose flour

1 cup (145 g) chopped and
    seeded fresh red bell
    pepper (½-inch pieces)

1 cup (145 g) cubed ham steak
    (½-inch pieces)

2 to 3 roughly chopped
    scallions (about ¾ cup
    [45 g]), both green and
    white parts, plus 1 finely
    chopped scallion for
    sprinkling postbake

1 cup (100 g) shredded
    Monterey Jack, divided

Spoonbread is in the cornbread family, but is its lighter, more pudding-like cousin. I love it warm when the cheese is still kind of melty and the texture is at its softest. Once cooled to room temperature, it firms up a bit and is still very tasty, but with a much more traditionally cornbread-like vibe. Red peppers are nice here, since the scallions are green, and you can even use jarred roasted ones, about ¾ cups (145 g), as does the always inspirational Melissa Clark in her spoonbread recipe.

───────

1. Heat the oven to 350°F. Grease an 8-inch square baking dish with cooking spray.

2. Whisk together the butter, heavy cream, sour cream, and eggs in a large bowl until combined. Vigorously whisk the baking powder, then the baking soda, into the egg mixture, and then whisk in the sugar, salt, black pepper, and cornmeal. Gently fold in the flour, peppers, ham, scallions, and ¾ cup (75 g) of the cheese, just until the last streak of flour disappears. Scrape the batter into the prepared pan and smooth the top.

3. Bake for about 35 minutes, sprinkling the top with the remaining ¼ cup (25 g) of cheese about 5 minutes before pulling the spoonbread from the oven. The bread is done when it is puffed, firm, and dry to the touch. Sprinkle with the finely chopped scallion and serve immediately from the baking dish, with a spoon.

VARIATION

For Easy "Mexican Street Corn" Spoonbread, reduce the salt to ½ teaspoon and the pepper to ¼ teaspoon, and add 1½ teaspoons chili-lime salt (see the Roasted Chili Lime Almonds, page 213, for a recipe) or Tajín along with the cornmeal. Substitute 1 cup (140 g) of frozen corn kernels for the bell pepper and omit the ham. Substitute 2 tablespoons of finely chopped fresh cilantro for the scallions, and 4 ounces (113 g) crumbled Cotija or feta for the Monterey Jack. Skip the sprinkle of extra cheese just before the bread is pulled from the oven, but do sprinkle with additional chopped cilantro, crumbled cheese, and an extra dusting of chili-lime salt postbake.

Zucchini Parm Scarpaccia

MAKES ONE 9-BY-13-INCH
SCARPACCIA
ACTIVE TIME: 15 MINUTES
BAKE TIME: 40 TO 45 MINUTES

3 large eggs

¾ cup (180 g) whole milk

1 cup (100 g) finely grated
Parmesan, plus more
for sprinkling

3 tablespoons olive oil, plus
more for drizzling prebake

¾ teaspoons kosher salt

½ teaspoon freshly ground
black pepper

¾ teaspoon red pepper flakes

1 teaspoon garlic powder

½ teaspoon onion powder

¾ cup (97 g) all-purpose flour

3 cups (390 g) grated zucchini
(about 2 medium unpeeled
zucchini)

1 cup (140 g) thinly sliced red
onion

Flaky sea salt for sprinkling

My Milwaukee-based pen pal, Kathy, introduced me to the world of scarpaccia and I couldn't be more excited to welcome you in, now. You might get loads o' frittata vibes from this dish, and I've also heard it referred to as a Dutch baby (which doesn't really resonate with me, though it *is* totes a custard-based dish) or a crustless tart or a sturdy, yet thin quiche. But no matter how it is described, to me all that matters is that it is incredibly tasty, calls for zuke—which I adore—and is as easy-peasy as they come. The salty finish of additional Parm and a few flakes of sea salt really makes this scarp pop.

1. Heat the oven to 400°F. Grease a 9-by-13-inch pan with cooking spray and line with a long piece of parchment that extends up and over the two long sides of the pan.

2. Whisk together the eggs, milk, Parmesan, oil, salt, black pepper, red pepper flakes, and garlic and onion powders in a large bowl. Whisk in the flour. Squeeze the grated zucchini in a clean dish towel or paper towels to release its liquid, and stir the zucchini and onion slices into the batter. Transfer to the prepared pan, drizzle with additional olive oil, and sprinkle with additional Parmesan.

3. Bake for 40 to 45 minutes, until nicely browned. Remove from the oven and sprinkle with flaky salt and a little extra Parmesan. Let cool for about 10 minutes before lifting out of the pan by the parchment overhang, running a butter knife around the short edges if it resists. Slice and serve warm or at room temperature.

CHAPTER 5

Breads You Need . . . But Don't Knead (Hee Hee Hee)

To say I was delighted when, many years ago, I made my first loaf of no-knead bread, is an understatement. I'd found the Jim Lahey recipe, adapted by Mark Bittman, in the *New York Times*, and at that time, I hardly even knew how to use yeast, let alone bake a loaf of homemade bread. Cut to a decade and a half later, when it came time to write the table of contents for this book, and I wondered about including a no-knead bread chapter. My first thought was absolutely not: How can I ask my beloved snackable bakers to wait a day to eat a loaf of bread? (No-knead bread typically requires 24 hours of fermentation.) But then I pondered whether I could create some *speedy* no-knead recipes. I thought maybe I could flavor and shape the breads in all sorts of interesting ways and that the recipes would be a welcome addition to an easy-peasy savory baking book, and ones that actually made perfect sense to include. And, spoiler alert: they do. The breads are as quick as no-knead bread can be, they are yeasty and chewy, and there is a different bread for every mood and occasion. Soft and Fluffy Buttery Rolls (page 154) for Thanksgiving; a Round and Crusty Bread for, well, for Jack and Oliver (page 150); Matt's Lard Bread (page 153) for lunch with a ball of fresh mozzarella and some thinly sliced prosciutto on the side; and Cheesiest Pepper Twirl Bread (page 158) for a late fall hang by the bonfire, beers in hand, with each person pulling off pieces of the still warm twirl as the sun sets. Anyway, you get the idea. This chapter rocks. 'Nuf said.

Pro Tips, Fun Facts, and Storing/Reheating Instructions

- I developed and tested these recipes in the summer, so when I say that **bread proofs more quickly in hot weather**, take it from me: I know from whence I speak. If your kitchen is toasty, like above 75°F, you might find your bread is ready to go in as little as 2 to 2½ hours.

- I find it is easiest to move the bread in and out of the pot that I bake it in by using **a parchment sling,** that you'll trim so its long sides are about the width of the bread.

- Although it takes a little bit of practice to **form your dough into a loose ball** after its long(ish) rise, you'll get the hang of it, I promise. Essentially, you want to place the dough on the counter in front of you—it will probably look like an oblong-shaped blob, but think of it as a round(ish) clock. First, pull the top of the dough at 12:00 down to the middle, then the bottom at 6:00 up to the middle. Then, pull the left side at 9:00 to the middle, overlapping the top and bottom pieces you just pulled, and

then pull the right side at 3:00 to the middle, overlapping the left (I owe this illustrative clock metaphor to my beloved and uber talented pal, Sam Seneviratne).

TO STORE: No-knead bread is best eaten the same day it is baked, fresh from the oven, but will last, tightly wrapped, overnight on the counter, or in the refrigerator if cheesy; or in the freezer for up to a month. Consider slicing before freezing to simplify enjoying one slice at a time. Although your future self will love you for it, I won't lie: I have never had the foresight to do the slicing-before-freezing thing, but here's to hoping you're a better person than I.

TO REHEAT: Reheat room-temperature bread, wrapped in foil, in a 300°F oven until warm, about 10 minutes. And not to throw too much at you here, but the Wonder(ful) Bread (page 161), the seeded boule (page 157), Matt's Lard Bread (page 153), and the Round and Crusty (page 150) can be sliced and toasted, rather than warmed in the oven, as well.

⚠ **WARNING:** Do Not Enter If You Are Incapable of Waiting 4 Hours to Eat Homemade Bread . . .

Round and Crusty Bread for Jack and Oliver

MAKES ONE 8-INCH BOULE
ACTIVE TIME: 5 MINUTES
REST TIME: 3 TO 3½ HOURS
BAKE TIME: 40 TO 50 MINUTES

3¼ cups (423 g) all-purpose flour, plus more for dusting

2¼ teaspoons instant yeast

2 teaspoons kosher salt

1½ cups (350 g) very warm, but not hot, water (about 110°F)

¼ teaspoon red wine vinegar

Inspired by Jim Lahey and Mark Bittman's "speedy no-knead bread," from their *New York Times* video, which calls for both "very warm water" and vinegar; as well as recipes by The Kitchn and my beloved pal Zoë François from her Bread in Five Minutes a Day cookbook series, this bread is what my children always referred to as "round and crusty." It's a flavorful, classic boule with a crumb of small, even holes. Reuse the plastic wrap that you'll need at two different times in the recipe, but be sure to flip it over the second time you use it, as one side will be covered in condensation.

1. Whisk together the flour, yeast, and salt in a large bowl. Pour in the warm water and vinegar, then stir with a flexible spatula until no loose flour remains and a sticky, rough dough forms. Cover the bowl with plastic wrap and place in a warmish spot until the dough doubles and the top is covered in small spongy-looking bubbles and air holes, 2½ to 3 hours, depending on the temperature of your kitchen.

2. Heat the oven to 450°F and place a covered 3½-quart Dutch oven inside it. Use a flexible bench scraper to scrape the sticky dough from the bowl onto a lightly floured piece of parchment paper. With floured hands, form it into a rough ball by pulling the top of the dough to the bottom, the bottom to the top, and one side over the other. Flip the dough over and let rest, covered with the plastic wrap, on the parchment for 30 minutes.

3. Peel off and discard the plastic wrap. Cut the width of the parchment so it is slightly wider than the dough, creating a vertical strip to lift the dough in and the bread out of the pot. Using pot holder–clad hands, carefully take the hot pot from the oven and remove the lid. Lift the dough up by the parchment and carefully place it in the pot. Secure the lid.

4. Bake for 30 minutes. Remove the lid and bake for 10 to 20 minutes longer, until the bread is bronzed and crispy, with an internal temperature of 190°F. Remove from the oven, carefully remove the bread from the pot, and let cool on a rack until room temperature before slicing and enjoying.

Matt's Lard Bread
WITH PROSCIUTTO, MOZZARELLA, AND BLACK PEPPER

My husband grew up in Massachusetts eating something called lard bread. I also grew up in Massachusetts but, sadly, my childhood diet included no such thing. Once we were married, however, Matt stumbled upon lard bread at an Italian bakery in Brooklyn, brought it home for me, and—of course—I adored it. At its simplest it is a bread studded with meat and cheese and often enriched with lard. My version here is studded with prosciutto and mozzarella and enriched with olive oil.

MAKES ONE 9-INCH BOULE
ACTIVE TIME: 10 MINUTES
REST TIME: 3 TO 3½ HOURS
BAKE TIME: 40 TO 50 MINUTES

3¼ cups (423 g) all-purpose flour, plus more for dusting

2¼ teaspoons instant yeast

2 teaspoons kosher salt

1½ teaspoons freshly ground black pepper

¾ cup plus 2 tablespoons (88 g) finely grated Parmesan or Pecorino Romano, at room temperature

6 ounces (170 g) prosciutto "steak," sliced ¼ inch thick and cubed, at room temperature, or Genoa salami, cut into ¼-inch cubes

1¼ cups (175 g) cubed low-moisture whole-milk mozzarella (¼-inch cubes), at room temperature

1½ cups (350 g) very warm, but not hot, water (about 110°F)

2 tablespoons olive oil

¼ teaspoon red wine vinegar

1. Whisk together the flour, yeast, salt, and pepper in a large bowl. Toss in the Parm, prosciutto, and mozzarella with your hands. Pour in the water, oil, and vinegar and stir with a flexible spatula until no loose flour remains. Cover the bowl with plastic wrap and place in a warmish spot until the dough doubles and the top is covered in small spongy-looking bubbles and air holes, 2½ to 3 hours.

2. Heat the oven to 450°F and place a covered 3½-quart Dutch oven inside it. Use a flexible bench scraper to scrape the sticky dough from the bowl onto a lightly floured piece of parchment paper. With floured hands, form it into a rough ball by pulling the top of the dough to the bottom, the bottom to the top, and one side over the other. Flip the dough over and let rest, covered with the plastic wrap, on the parchment for 30 minutes.

3. Peel off the plastic wrap. Cut the width of the parchment so it is slightly wider than the dough. Using pot holder–clad hands, carefully take the hot pot from the oven and remove the lid. Lift the dough up by the parchment and carefully place it in the pot. Secure the lid.

4. Bake for 30 minutes. Remove the lid and bake for 10 to 20 minutes longer, until the bread is bronzed, with an internal temp of 190°F. Remove the pot from the oven and carefully lift out the bread. Let cool on a rack for 10 minutes before slicing and enjoying warm.

Soft and Fluffy Buttery Rolls

A cross between a Parker House roll and a crusty dinner roll, these have soft and fluffy insides and slightly crispy tops. Assembled in two 8-inch round pans, they bake up looking like many-petaled flowers and can be pulled apart right at the table, revealing their pillowy sides.

MAKES 16 ROLLS

ACTIVE TIME: 10 MINUTES

REST TIME: 2 HOURS 45 MINUTES

BAKE TIME: 25 TO 30 MINUTES

3¼ cups (423 g) all-purpose flour, plus more for dusting

2¼ teaspoons instant yeast

2 teaspoons kosher salt

1½ cups (360 g) very warm, but not hot, whole milk (about 110°F)

½ cup (113 g) unsalted butter, melted, divided

1 large egg, beaten, at room temperature

The Ultimate Egg Wash (page 230)

1. Whisk together the flour, yeast, and salt in a large bowl. Pour in the milk, ¼ cup (56 g) of the melted butter, and the beaten egg and stir with a flexible spatula until a wettish dough forms. Cover the bowl with plastic wrap and place in a warm-ish spot, until the dough is puffed, airy, and doubled, and the top has some visible bubbles, about 2 hours.

2. Grease two 8-inch round pans with cooking spray. Use a flex-ible bench scraper to scrape the sticky dough from the bowl onto a lightly floured work surface. With floured hands, form it into a rough ball by pulling the top of the dough to the bot-tom, the bottom to the top, and one side over the other. Flip it over, sprinkle your work surface with a little more flour, and pat the dough into a rectangle, about 8 by 12-inches.

3. Divide the dough into 16 pieces (about 55 g each). Form each piece into a ball, by first tucking under its edges and then plac-ing it on your floured surface, cupping one hand around it and moving it in a circular motion so that its bottom drags on the floured surface. Place eight balls in each prepared pan and let rest, covered for 45 minutes. Heat the oven to 400°F.

4. Brush the dough with egg wash and bake for 25 to 30 minutes, rotating and brushing with half of the remaining melted but-ter at the halfway point, until nicely bronzed. Remove from the oven, brush a final time with butter, and serve.

Seeded Olive Oil Whole Wheat Boule

I won't lie: I'm more of a white bread girl than a whole wheat one; but I make an exception when it comes to this here boule. It makes the perfect toast to soak up runny eggs in the morning, and is lovely served at a dinner party, sliced thickly, wrapped in a tea towel, and tucked in a bread basket—with softened salted butter on the side, natch.

MAKES ONE 8-INCH BOULE
ACTIVE TIME: 5 MINUTES
REST TIME: 3 TO 3½ HOURS
BAKE TIME: 40 TO 50 MINUTES

2¼ cups (292 g) all-purpose flour, plus more for dusting

1 cup (120 g) whole wheat flour

3 tablespoons raw sunflower seeds, plus more for sprinkling

3 tablespoons pumpkin seeds (aka pepitas), plus more for sprinkling

2 tablespoons white sesame seeds, plus more for sprinkling

1 tablespoon black sesame seeds, plus more for sprinkling

2¼ teaspoons instant yeast

2 teaspoons kosher salt

1½ cups (350 g) very warm, but not hot, water (about 110°F)

¼ cup (50 g) olive oil

2 tablespoons honey

¼ teaspoon red wine vinegar

1. Whisk together the flours, seeds, yeast, and salt in a large bowl. Pour in the water, oil, honey, and vinegar and stir with a flexible spatula until no loose flour remains and a sticky, rough dough forms. Cover the bowl with plastic wrap and place in a warmish spot until the dough doubles and the top is covered in small spongy-looking bubbles and air holes, 2½ to 3 hours, depending on the temperature of your kitchen.

2. Heat the oven to 450°F and place a covered 3½-quart Dutch oven inside it. Use a flexible bench scraper to scrape the sticky dough from the bowl onto a lightly floured piece of parchment paper. With floured hands, form it into a rough ball by pulling the top of the dough to the bottom, the bottom to the top, and one side over the other. Flip the dough over and decoratively sprinkle with additional seeds. Let rest, covered with the plastic wrap, on the parchment for 30 minutes.

3. Peel off and discard the plastic wrap. Cut the width of the parchment so it is only slightly wider than the dough. Using pot holder–clad hands, carefully take the hot pot from the oven and remove the lid. Lift the dough up by the parchment and carefully place it in the pot. Secure the lid.

4. Bake for 30 minutes. Remove the lid and bake for 10 to 20 minutes longer, until the bread is bronzed and crispy, with an internal temperature of 190°F. Carefully remove the bread from the pot and let cool on a rack until room temperature before slicing and enjoying.

Cheesiest Pepper Twirl Bread

If a grilled cheese sandwich and a babka had a baby, I'm pretty sure it would look and taste a lot like this cheesiest pepper bread. It's soft and fluffy with loads o' gooey cheese pockets. Extremely delicious and def best served warm.

MAKES ONE 9-INCH ROUND BREAD
ACTIVE TIME: 10 MINUTES
REST TIME: 2 HOURS 45 MINUTES
BAKE TIME: 45 MINUTES

3¼ cups (423 g) all-purpose flour, plus more for dusting

2¼ teaspoons instant yeast

2 teaspoons kosher salt

1½ cups (360 g) very warm, but not hot, whole milk (about 110°F)

¼ cup (56 g) unsalted butter, melted

1 large egg, beaten, at room temperature

Mayonnaise for brushing

3 cups (300 g) shredded pepper Jack cheese, for a peppery vibe, or Monterey Jack or Muenster for a milder flavor

The Ultimate Egg Wash (page 230)

1. Whisk together the flour, yeast, and salt in a large bowl. Pour in the milk, melted butter, and beaten egg and stir with a flexible spatula until a wettish dough forms. Cover the bowl with plastic wrap and place in a warmish spot, until the dough is puffed, airy, and doubled and the top has some visible bubbles, about 2 hours.

2. Grease a 9-inch round pan with cooking spray. Use a flexible bench scraper to scrape the sticky dough from the bowl onto a generously floured work surface. With floured hands, form it into a rough ball by pulling the top of the dough to the bottom, the bottom to the top, and one side over the other. Flip it over, sprinkle your work surface with a little more flour, and with a well-floured rolling pin, roll the dough into a rectangle, about 12 by 16 inches, with the long side facing you.

3. Brush with mayonnaise, leaving a 1-inch bare border around all sides. Evenly sprinkle the cheese over the mayonnaise, lightly pressing it down with your hands to adhere. From one of the long sides, roll the rectangle into a tight, even log. Pinch the seam and two ends to seal. Place the log seam side down and, stretch the log until it is 24 to 30 inches long. Twist the log into a coil and place in the pan. Don't worry if it doesn't entirely cover the pan's bottom—it will expand as it proofs. Let rest, covered, for about 45 minutes, or until the dough has doubled in size. Heat the oven to 350°F.

4. Brush the dough with egg wash and bake for 45 minutes, rotating at the halfway point, until bronzed, with an internal temp of 190°F. Remove the bread from the pan, let rest for 10 minutes, and serve.

Wonder(ful) Bread

MAKES ONE 8½-BY-4½-INCH LOAF
ACTIVE TIME: 5 MINUTES
REST TIME: 3 TO 3½ HOURS
BAKE TIME: 30 MINUTES

3¼ cups (423 g) all-purpose flour, plus more for dusting

2¼ teaspoons instant yeast

2 teaspoons kosher salt

1½ cups (350 g) very warm, but not hot, water (about 110°F)

¼ teaspoon red wine vinegar

The Ultimate Egg Wash (page 230)

Although (tragically) neither my mother nor father ever purchased Wonder Bread for me and my brother when we were growing up, I ate it frequently at the homes of friends whose parents were far nicer than mine—and because it was forbidden in my house, I coveted every squishy slice. This bread is my homemade/grown-up version of the Wonder Bread of my childhood. It is very yeasty with a tight, spongy crumb. PB&J never had it this good.

1. Whisk together the flour, yeast, and salt in a large bowl. Pour in the water and vinegar and stir with a flexible spatula until no loose flour remains. Cover the bowl with plastic wrap and place in a warmish spot until the dough doubles and the top is covered in small spongy-looking bubbles and air holes, 2½ to 3 hours.

2. Heat the oven to 450°F. Grease an 8½-by-4½-inch loaf pan with cooking spray. Use a flexible bench scraper to scrape the sticky dough from the bowl onto a lightly floured work surface and knead it three to five times. Sprinkle your work surface with a bit of extra flour and pat the dough into a rectangle, about 6 by 8 inches. From one of the longer sides, roll it into a tight, even log, pinching the seam and the two ends to seal. Place the log, seam side down, in the prepared pan. Don't worry if it doesn't cover the entire bottom of the pan—it will expand as it proofs. Let rest, covered with plastic wrap, for about 30 minutes, until the dough has doubled in size and just crowns the top of the pan.

3. Peel off and discard the plastic wrap. Brush the top of the dough with egg wash, prick any air bubbles that have formed with a wooden skewer, and score it with a sharp paring knife, making a single cut down the middle.

4. Bake for 30 minutes, or until the bread is nicely bronzed, with an internal temperature of 190°F. Remove from the pan and let cool on a rack until room temperature before slicing and PB&J-ing up a storm.

Anchovy Onion Pizza

MAKES ONE 9-BY-13-INCH PIZZA
ACTIVE TIME: 10 MINUTES
REST TIME: 3 TO 3½ HOURS
BAKE TIME: ABOUT 35 MINUTES

3¼ cups (423 g) all-purpose flour, plus more for dusting

2¼ teaspoons instant yeast

2 teaspoons kosher salt

1½ cups (350 g) very warm, but not hot, water (about 110 °F)

½ cup (100 g) olive oil, divided, plus more for the pan and drizzling

¼ teaspoon red wine vinegar

1 teaspoon dried thyme

1 teaspoon garlic powder

½ teaspoon onion powder

¼ cup (40 g) finely chopped anchovy fillets

One batch Quickest (Yet Tastiest) Caramelized Onions (page 237), room temperature

VARIATION

For Marinara Pizza, substitute 1 teaspoon dried oregano, ½ teaspoon red pepper flakes, ½ teaspoon garlic powder for herbs and spices in the oil. Omit anchovies and onions. Bake 20 mins, spread with ¾ cup (191 g) marinara sauce, leaving ½ inch bare border. Bake 25 mins more. Sprinkle with ½ cup (50 g) Parm and serve.

This delightful bread is akin to focaccia, but with an anchovy and onion topping inspired by a Provençale dish called *pissaladière*. Now, whether any of that interests you or not, I can't say, so let me just cut to the chase and inform you that this soft and chewy bread, coupled with the jammy, sweet onions and the salty, fishy anchovies, is just exactly what you want to be eating as often as you can get away with, as will anyone you're willing to share it with.

1. Whisk together the flour, yeast, and salt in a large bowl. Pour in the water, ¼ cup (50 g) of the olive oil, and the vinegar and stir with a flexible spatula until no loose flour remains and a sticky, rough dough forms. Cover the bowl with plastic wrap and place in a warmish spot until the dough doubles and the top is covered in small spongy-looking bubbles and air holes, 2½ to 3 hours, depending on the temperature of your kitchen.

2. Heat the oven to 400°F. Grease a 9-by-13-inch metal baking pan with olive oil. Use a flexible bench scraper to scrape the sticky dough from the bowl onto a lightly floured work surface. With floured hands, form it into a rough ball by pulling the top of the dough to the bottom, the bottom to the top, and one side over the other. Flip the dough over and transfer it to the prepared pan, using your fingers to nudge the dough into the corners. Let rest, covered with the plastic wrap, for 30 minutes.

3. Peel off and discard the plastic wrap. Whisk the thyme and garlic and onion powders into the remaining ¼ cup (50 g) olive oil in a small bowl. Dip your fingertips in the seasoned oil and dimple the dough all over, as you would when making focaccia. Brush the rest of the oil over the dough, then decoratively and evenly arrange the anchovies and onions on top.

4. Bake for about 35 minutes, rotating at the halfway point, until the edges are bronzed and crispy. Remove from the oven, drizzle with additional olive oil, and use a metal spatula to carefully slide the pizza out of the pan and onto a cooling rack. Let cool about 10 minutes before slicing and enjoying.

CHAPTER 6

Savory Cookies and Easy Crackers

For me, salty, cheesy, herby, crispy cookies are a complete revelation. I mean, who knew you could put stinky, yummy, creamy gorgonzola in cookies, fill them with fig jam and become the most popular person in your neighborhood? Or put loads of cheddar and paprika in biscotti and literally create something that tastes like a grown-up Cheez-it? Or make homemade matzos, with the most gorgeous hue, that are utterly addictive? Cream Cheese and Olive Pinwheels (page 172) are literally my everything cause life is nothing without cream cheese and olive sandwiches. And Nonnie's Crackers in the Oven (page 188) give all the nostalgic feels to my husband and boys—who ever said no to a sentimental cracker? All the cookies and crackers work beautifully on a cheese plate or "board" and are also nice with a late-night glass of wine or a beer. I mean, I could go on and on, but do we really need a reason, situation or location to eat a cookie/cracker?

Pro Tips, Fun Facts, and Storing/Reheating Instructions

- There is a little more resting happening prebake when savory cookies and easy crackers are on the snackable baking agenda. And, basically, I blame my beloved cheese for the need to rest cookies (t's just a melty little bugger, and when you add it to cookie dough, the dough needs chilling before baking, to prevent spreading) and I blame pesky old gluten for the need to rest crackers (they are easier to roll super-thin after the gluten has had time to relax). But here's the thing: cookie and cracker assembly is so darn fast that the chilling is truly a mere blip in the journey to eating the treats in this chapter. And a blip that results in a tasty cheesy or crispy treat, has "worth it" written all over it, right?

- **People go crazy for the Gorgonzola Fig Jam Drops (page 168)**, and I both get it, and don't. Like, who knew everyone loved blue cheese in cookies?! Anyway, consider yourself warned.

- **Fire Crackers (page 184) are fiery**—there are no two ways about it, and I'd pull back a little on the red pepper flakes if that could be problematic for you.

- Oh, and **peeps also go ballistic for the Butter Crackers with Melty Cheese and Sour Pickles (page 187)**. I mean, it happened to me—that thing where you can't stop eating something even though you know you should.

- Depending on how pro-seed you are, the Seedy Sesame Crackers with Oats (page 183) might read too "healthy" to you. I mean, in a contest between a "good for you" cracker and the aforementioned butter crackers (and can we just call a spade a spade and admit we're talking about Ritz?), the latter kind are winning every time. But folks, **these Seedy Sesame Crackers are fantastically salty and crunchy and gorgeous and fun to make** (I mean, flax-seeds' ability to bind these cuties together is weirdly magical). And if your oats are gluten free, well then, these crackers are gluten-free, too. Surprising as it may seem, these seed-filled treasures could very well end up a fan favorite.

TO STORE: Savory cookies and easy crackers are best eaten the day they are made, but will last 3 to 5 days in an airtight container on the counter (save for the following exceptions), or in the freezer for up to a month.

- The pinwheel cookies can be stored overnight in the refrigerator or frozen for up to a month.
- The butter crackers with pickles do not last—and yes: this is indeed a tragedy.

TO REHEAT: Only the pinwheels need reheating. Do so with room temperature wheels on a parchment-lined baking sheet in a 300°F oven until warm, 5 to 10 minutes.

Gorgonzola Fig Jam Drops

MAKES 25 COOKIES
ACTIVE TIME: 10 MINUTES
REST TIME: 30 MINUTES
BAKE TIME: 16 TO 18 MINUTES

¾ teaspoon kosher salt

¼ teaspoon freshly ground black pepper

½ cup (113 g) unsalted butter, melted and cooled slightly

1¾ cups (225 g) Gorgonzola or another soft blue cheese, crumbled, at room temperature

1¼ cups (162 g) all-purpose flour

⅓ cup (67 g) granulated sugar for rolling

½ cup (160 g) fig jam

VARIATION

For Cheddar and Hot Pepper Jelly Drops, add ¼ teaspoon of paprika and ¼ teaspoon of garlic powder to the seasonings in the melted butter. Substitute 2 cups (200 g) shredded Cheddar for the Gorgonzola, and hot pepper jelly for the fig jam. The dough will be a tad crumblier than the Gorgonzola version, so you may need to knead it a bit to bring it together. Hold the balls in your hand, rather than leaving them on the baking sheet, when indenting them.

Blue cheese cookies for the win, as the combo of the funky Gorgonzola with the sweet figgy jam is just so damn good. Rolling the cookies in sugar prebake plays up the sweet and salty elements of these drops, though they are still very savory. If you can stand it, a longer rest time, about an hour or so, results in slightly more shapely drops. These are an excellent addition to a cheese board and people will worship you when you serve them (been there, done that). The Cheddar hot pepper jelly variation is divine, as well, and inspired by an Allrecipes recipe.

1. Line two baking sheets with parchment paper.

2. Whisk the salt and pepper into the melted butter in a medium bowl. Stir in the cheese with a flexible spatula, smooshing it into the seasoned butter until combined, then fold in the flour. Place the sugar in a small bowl. Form the dough into 1-inch balls (about a scant 1-tablespoon each [15 g]), roll them in the sugar, then place them on one of the prepared baking sheets. Use the handle of a wooden spoon or another dowel-shaped tool to make an indentation about ½ inch deep in the top of each ball and then use your finger to make each hole a little wider and deeper. Fill each hole with ½ teaspoon of jam (you may have a bit of jam leftover). Freeze the cookies for at least 30 minutes and heat the oven to 375°F.

3. Equally divide the frozen cookies between the two prepared baking sheets. Bake for 16 to 18 minutes, rotating and swapping the placement of the sheets at the halfway point, until nicely browned. Remove from the oven and let cool to room temperature before serving.

Jalapeño Cheddar Shortbread Buttons

These spicy buttons, with their vinegary jalapeño kick coupled with the creamy sharp Cheddar is exactly what you didn't know you needed for an afternoon tea break when working from home—or as a last-minute gift when headed to a friend's for drinks or dinner. Yes, they require at least a 30-minute rest, and yes, I'm sorry for that . . . but even with as much as a 45-minute one, you'll be pulling buttons from the oven within about an hour of assembling them. Speedy says, as speedy does. I like sharp white Cheddar here, as opposed to orange, but you do you.

MAKES 40 TO 45 BUTTONS

ACTIVE TIME: 10 MINUTES

REST TIME: AT LEAST 30 MINUTES

BAKE TIME: ABOUT 30 MINUTES

1 cup (226 g) unsalted butter, melted and cooled slightly

½ teaspoon kosher salt

¼ teaspoon freshly ground black pepper

2 cups (200 g) shredded white sharp Cheddar

¼ cup plus 2 tablespoons (67 g) coarsely chopped pickled sliced jalapeños

2 cups (260 g) all-purpose flour

1. Line two baking sheets with parchment paper.

2. Whisk together the melted butter, salt, and black pepper in a large bowl. Fold in the cheese and jalapeños, and then the flour with a flexible spatula, just until the last streak of flour disappears. Scoop the dough into 1-tablespoon (14 g) mounds using a portion scoop, if you have one, or a measuring spoon—you do not need to roll them into balls, as, fun fact, perfectly shaped buttons are actually flat on the bottom.

3. Place them on one of the prepared baking sheets and freeze for a minimum of 30 minutes. The baked buttons may have a tiny bit of cheese leakage if only rested for 30 minutes and will (annoyingly) retain their shape the best after 60—but you are a busy peep and if you need to stop resting at 30, you have my blessing.

4. Heat the oven to 350°F. Equally divide the frozen buttons between the two prepared baking sheets. Bake for about 30 minutes, rotating and swapping the placement of the sheets at the halfway point, until lightly browned. Remove from the oven and let cool to room temperature before serving.

Cream Cheese and Olive Pinwheels

Cream cheese and olive sandwiches on soft white bread, crusts removed, and cut in triangles, give me all the tangy, umami, creamy, briny feels. And so when developing a savory pinwheel cookie for you, made from my Best-Ever Cream Biscuit Dough (page 234)—that already tastes like a cushiony bread—the ingredients of my fave tea party sandwich seemed like exactly the right move.

MAKES 26 PINWHEELS
ACTIVE TIME: 15 MINUTES
REST TIME: 20 MINUTES
BAKE TIME: 20 MINUTES PER SHEET

8 ounces (227 g) full-fat cream cheese, at room temperature

½ teaspoon kosher salt

½ teaspoon freshly ground black pepper

1 teaspoon garlic powder

All-purpose flour for dusting

One batch Best-Ever Cream Biscuit Dough (page 234)

1¼ cups (180 g) drained small pimiento-stuffed olives, coarsely chopped, brine reserved for brushing

The Ultimate Egg Wash (page 230)

1. Heat the oven to 425°F. Line two baking sheets with parchment paper.

2. Combine the cream cheese, salt, pepper, and garlic powder in a small bowl, using a fork.

3. Dump the biscuit dough onto a floured work surface and knead gently to bring it together. With floured hands, pat the dough into a rectangle. Using a rolling pin, roll the dough into a 10-by-16-inch rectangle with the long side facing you. Spread the cream cheese mixture over the dough, leaving a ½- to 1-inch bare border on all sides.

4. Sprinkle the olives over the cream cheese, pressing down lightly to adhere. Starting from the long edge of the rectangle farthest from you, begin tightly rolling up the dough toward you—it'll be squishy and a little hard to work with. Pinch the dough to seal the seam, flip the log so it is seam side down, trim the ends, and cut the log in half. Gently stretch each log until 13 inches long and freeze for 10 minutes.

5. Remove one log from the freezer, and with a chef's knife, slice into thirteen 1-inch-wide pieces, rotating the log as you work. Place them on one of the prepared baking sheets and use your hands to reshape and flatten them slightly. Brush each pinwheel with egg wash and place the sheet in the freezer for 10 minutes. Repeat with the remaining log.

6. Bake, one sheet at a time, for about 20 minutes, until the wheels are lightly browned. Remove from the oven, immediately brush with reserved olive brine, and serve.

Scottish(ish) Oat Cakes

MAKES 8 OAT CAKES
ACTIVE TIME: 5 MINUTES
BAKE TIME: 25 TO 30 MINUTES

1 cup (100 g) quick one-minute oats, plus more for dusting

½ cup (65 g) all-purpose flour

2 teaspoons packed light brown sugar

¼ teaspoon baking soda

½ teaspoon kosher salt

¼ cup (56 g) unsalted butter, melted and cooled slightly

3 tablespoons hot water

Honestly, I was not expecting to be quite so taken with these cute little cakes. I wanted to include a recipe for them, as they are easy and folks seem to dig them, but didn't really get how truly special they are until I baked up a batch. They are very slightly sweet, very oatty, crumbly, and just perfect with a slice of cheese and maybe a pickle; or even a smear of cream cheese and a little lox. Pro tip: Microwave the butter and water together, and once the butter melts, the water will be hot and you'll be good to go.

1. Heat the oven to 350°F. Line a baking sheet with parchment paper.

2. Whisk together the oats, flour, brown sugar, baking soda, and salt in a medium bowl. Pour in the melted butter and water and stir with a flexible spatula to combine.

3. Lightly sprinkle a work surface with oats and divide the dough into eight small balls (about 32 g each). Press the balls into the sprinkled oats to coat, and then flatten them into 3-inch-diameter cakes (you can flip them over to coat both sides, or just do one side). Use your fingers to smooth any cracked edges.

4. Place the cakes on the prepared baking sheet and bake for 25 to 30 minutes, rotating at the halfway point, until lightly browned. Remove from the oven and serve warm or at room temperature.

Cheeziest Biscotti

MAKES ABOUT 20 BISCOTTI
ACTIVE TIME: 10 MINUTES
REST TIME: 30 MINUTES
BAKE TIME: 60 TO 65 MINUTES

½ cup (113 g) unsalted butter,
    melted and cooled slightly
2 tablespoons granulated
    sugar
2 cups (200 g) shredded
    Cheddar
2 large eggs, at room
    temperature
2 teaspoons baking powder
1 teaspoon kosher salt
1 teaspoon paprika
½ teaspoon cayenne pepper
2 cups (260 g) all-purpose flour
The Ultimate Egg Wash
    (page 230)
Flaky sea salt for sprinkling

I am a sucker for a baked good that tastes like—and is named after—a grocery-store snack, so it should come as no surprise that these *cheeziest* (aka Cheez-it) biscotti are up there on my list of fave "sav-ookies" (aka savory cookies). These are crazy easy to assemble but like all biscotti, they *do* need to be baked twice and be brought to room temperature in between each bake. Less than ideal, I know. But here's a time-saving pro tip: To speed things up after the first bake, freeze the logs for 15 minutes rather than leaving them on the counter, for 30. Oh, and instead of serving buttered toast "soldiers" with your eggs, try one of these cheezy soldierlike *cookies*, instead.

1. Heat the oven to 350°F. Line a baking sheet with parchment paper.

2. Whisk the melted butter and sugar together in a large bowl. Whisk in the cheese and then the eggs, one at a time. Vigorously whisk in the baking powder, and then the salt, paprika, and cayenne. Fold in the flour with a flexible spatula.

3. Divide the dough in half (about 350 g each), and transfer to the prepared pan. Shape the dough into two logs about 10 inches long and about 2 inches wide. Brush the logs with the egg wash and sprinkle with flaky salt.

4. Bake until dry-looking and lightly browned, about 30 minutes. Remove from the oven, let the logs cool for 30 minutes, trim the ends, then slice them about ¾ inch thick with a serrated knife, using a gentle sawing motion. Set the slices upright on the same baking sheet.

5. Bake the sliced biscotti again for 30 to 35 minutes, until the sides look dried and browned. Remove from the oven and let cool to room temperature before serving.

Crumbly Gouda Bites

MAKES 36 BITES
ACTIVE TIME: 10 MINUTES
BAKE TIME: 40 TO 50 MINUTES

½ teaspoon cayenne pepper, plus more for sprinkling

½ teaspoon kosher salt

¼ teaspoon freshly ground black pepper

½ cup (113 g) unsalted butter, melted and cooled slightly

2⅓ cups (233 g) shredded Gouda, or your fave

1 cup (130 g) all-purpose flour

Flaky sea salt for sprinkling

A little crumbly, with slightly soft cheesy middles (due to the high ratio of cheese to flour) and crispy, almost fried cheese-like tops, these buttery bites are the savory little sisters of the tiny lavender bites from *Snackable Bakes*. Use a soft Gouda with red wax, as opposed to an aged one, and have at it with the cayenne postbake, depending on how zesty (or not) you're feeling. These cuties don't *love* being sliced into adorable little squares—they crumble and the edges aren't as sharp as we sharp-edge lovers would like—but wildly addictive they are, and I hope you'll agree that's really all we care about when biting our bites.

1. Heat the oven to 350°F. Line an 8-inch square pan with a long sheet of parchment paper that extends up and over two opposite sides of the pan.

2. Whisk the cayenne, salt, and black pepper into the melted butter in a medium bowl. Stir in the cheese with a flexible spatula, and then the flour just until the last streak of flour disappears. Scrape the dough into the prepared pan and press it into the bottom with your hands. Sprinkle with extra cayenne and flaky salt.

3. Bake for 40 to 50 minutes, until the bites are lightly browned and are pulling away from the sides of the pan. Remove from the oven and let cool to room temperature, then lift from the pan with the parchment overhang, running a knife around the edges if it resists. Cut the slab into 36 small square bites and serve.

Olive Oil Thyme Crackers
WITH FLAKY SEA SALT

Blistered, fragrant, salty, and beyond crispy, these crackers are my everything. I like baking them in sheets and breaking them postbake by hand, but you can cut them into shapes prebake, if you'd like. Because these are baked one sheet of crackers at a time, the second batch may be easier to work with and end up a tad crisper than the first, due to the rest. So, yes, if the crispiest of crackers is your goal, you can rest all of the dough for up to 30 or 40 minutes before rolling it out.

MAKES 2 LARGE CRACKERS
FOR BREAKING

ACTIVE TIME: 10 MINUTES

REST TIME: 20 MINUTES

BAKE TIME: 20 MINUTES FOR
EACH LARGE CRACKER

2 cups (260 g) all-purpose flour

1 teaspoon baking powder

1 teaspoon kosher salt

2 teaspoons dried thyme, plus
more for sprinkling

⅔ cup (155 g) water

¼ cup (50 g) olive oil, plus more
for brushing prebake

Flaky sea salt for sprinkling

1. Heat the oven to 425°F. Have ready two baking sheets.

2. Whisk together the flour, baking powder, salt, and thyme in a large bowl. Pour in the water and oil and stir. Knead the dough in the bowl until a soft, smooth(ish) ball forms. Cover the bowl with a clean dish towel and let rest for 20 minutes.

3. Divide the dough equally in half (about 235 g each), and place one piece between two sheets of parchment paper (leave the other portion covered in the bowl). Roll out the dough as thinly as possible (thin dough = crispy crackers), peeling back the top paper and continuously stretching the edges of the dough with your fingers. Peel off the top piece of paper, brush the dough with olive oil, and sprinkle with flaky salt and thyme. Roll out the dough once or twice more, so the thyme and salt adhere to the dough. Lift the dough plus paper onto one of the baking sheets.

4. Bake for 10 minutes, then remove the baking sheet from the oven and carefully flip the cracker over—if you do it quickly, it won't burn your fingers. Return the pan to the oven and bake for 10 minutes more, until dry, crispy, and browned around the edges.

5. Repeat with the other piece of dough. Let cool to room temp before breaking into pieces and serving.

Seedy Sesame Crackers
WITH OATS

MAKES 1 LARGE CRACKER FOR BREAKING
ACTIVE TIME: 5 MINUTES
REST TIME: 15 TO 20 MINUTES
BAKE TIME: 30 TO 35 MINUTES

¼ cup (25 g) quick one-minute oats

¼ cup (35 g) raw pumpkin seeds (aka pepitas)

¼ cup (35 g) sesame seeds, black, white, or both

¼ cup (40 g) flaxseeds

¾ teaspoon kosher salt

½ teaspoon garlic powder

¼ teaspoon onion powder

¼ teaspoon cayenne pepper

½ cup (116 g) boiling water

Flaky sea salt for sprinkling

Wow: who knew that (a) I could develop such fantastic, light and crispy seed crackers (that are gluten-free to boot, if you use GF oats); and (b) that I would be so fond of them. They're crazy snackable—like popcorn (I just keep breaking off pieces and popping them in my mouth). The cayenne gives them bite, which to me is always a good thing. Use black sesame seeds, rather than white, for the best-looking crackers—or go to town and use both.

1. Heat the oven to 350°F. Line a baking sheet with parchment paper.

2. Whisk together the oats, pumpkin seeds, sesame seeds, flax-seeds, salt, garlic and onion powders, and cayenne in a large bowl. Pour in the water and stir with a flexible spatula to combine. Cover with a clean dish towel and let sit for 15 to 20 minutes so the flax can work its gelling magic.

3. Stir the mixture once or twice to ensure all the water has been absorbed, and then dump it onto the prepared baking sheet. Using your flexible spatula, spread the mixture as evenly as you can over the bottom of the pan—it won't reach all the corners, but will cover most of it.

4. Sprinkle with flaky salt and bake for 30 to 35 minutes, rotating at the halfway point, until the cracker is lightly browned and crispy. Remove from the oven and let cool to room temperature before breaking into pieces and serving.

Fire Crackers

MAKES 70 CRACKERS
ACTIVE TIME: 5 MINUTES
REST TIME: AT LEAST 1 HOUR
BAKE TIME: 10 TO 15 MINUTES

¼ cup (35 g) buttermilk powder

1 teaspoon onion powder

1 teaspoon garlic powder

1 teaspoon dried parsley

1 teaspoon dried dill

1 teaspoon dried chives

½ teaspoon kosher salt

¼ teaspoon freshly ground
    black pepper

1½ to 2 tablespoons red pepper
    flakes; use the smaller
    amount if you're feeling
    only moderately fiery

1 cup (200 g) olive oil

2 sleeves (227 g) saltines or
    soda crackers (about
    70 crackers)

VARIATION

For "Pizza Crackers," replace
the buttermilk powder with
2 tablespoons of nutritional
yeast, and reduce the onion
powder to 1 teaspoon. Substitute 1 tablespoon of Italian
seasoning for the parsley, dill,
and chives. Increase the salt
by ½ teaspoon and proceed
with the recipe as written.

Fire crackers are new to me and I'm just thrilled that we've been introduced. For the uninitiated, a fire cracker is a saltine cracker that's been soaked in seasoned oil overnight and then baked. Traditionally, the seasoning is ranch-inspired, and in fact, a typical recipe includes two packets of ranch seasoning. We're going the from scratch route here, with some buttermilk powder and ranch-friendly spices, which means that homemade ranch seasoning is now in your wheelhouse and I couldn't be more proud of you. However, you can substitute the store-bought stuff if you would like. The crackers *can* marinate in the seasoned oil overnight, but who has time for that?

1. Whisk together everything but the oil and saltines in a medium bowl. Whisk in the oil. Place the crackers in a resealable plastic bag (the crackers will settle on the bottom of the bag, weighing it down and allowing the bag to easily sit, zipped side open, on the counter). Pour in the seasoned oil, seal the bag, and gently shake to coat, turning the bag over a few times, until all the crackers are covered. Lay the bag on its side and let the crackers soak up the seasoned oil for at least an hour, flipping the bag over every 15 minutes, and up to overnight.

2. Heat the oven to 325°F. Have ready two parchment-lined baking sheets.

3. Place the crackers in a single layer on the two prepared sheets, scraping out the excess "topping" from the bag with your fingers and sprinkling it over/rubbing it into the crackers as best you can (it's messy work, but someone has to do it).

4. Bake for 10 to 15 minutes, rotating the sheets at the halfway point and swapping their placement in the oven, until the crackers are fragrant and lightly browned. Remove from the oven and let cool for at least 5 minutes before serving.

Butter Crackers
WITH MELTY CHEESE AND SOUR PICKLES

MAKES 32 CRACKERS
ACTIVE TIME: 5 MINUTES
BAKE TIME: 5 MINUTES

3 to 4 deli-style sour pickles

7 to 8 ounces Monterey Jack, preferably in a rectangular block

1 sleeve (105 g) butter crackers, such as Ritz brand (about 32 crackers)

These baked butter crackers (aka Ritz) topped with cheese and pickles are inspired (in kind of a roundabout way) by Gabrielle Hamilton's *New York Times* recipe for fried saltines with Cheddar and onions. You see, I'd originally intended to fry up a bunch of crackers for this recipe, just as Gabrielle instructs. But then reality hit and I realized that I wasn't really up for frying crackers in an easy-peasy baking book, plus Nonnie's Crackers in the Oven (page 188) give you all the fried cracker vibes you're going to need. But baking them with cheese and pickles? Sign me up. I did a quick Google search to see whether anyone else had ever thought to do something as genius as combining butter crackers, cheese, and pickles. And wouldn't you know it, "pickle cookies" turned out to be a TikTok thing. Oh, well. No good deed . . . and all that.

1. Heat the oven to 350°F. Line a baking sheet with parchment paper.

2. Slice the pickles into thirty-two ¼- to ⅜-inch-thick coins and the cheese into thirty-two ¼-inch-thick squares large enough to cover the pickle slices with some overhang. Place the crackers in a single layer on the prepared baking sheet. Top each with a slice of pickle and then a slice of cheese.

3. Bake for 5 minutes, or until the cheese is melted and soft. Remove from the oven and let cool briefly. Serve warm.

4. These don't really keep, so consuming the entire batch with your besties in one sitting, is highly encouraged.

Nonnie's Crackers in the Oven

MAKES 35 CRACKERS
ACTIVE TIME: 5 MINUTES
BAKE TIME: 10 MINUTES

1 sleeve (113 g) saltines or
    soda crackers (about
    35 crackers)
½ cup (113 g) unsalted
    butter, melted

Although these crackers in the oven are nothing more than crackers dunked in butter and baked, they taste as if they've been fried; and buttery, crispy *fried* crackers are literally a thing of beauty. My MIL made crackers in the oven for breakfast for my husband when he was little, and then for our two boys and their 19 cousins (yes: it's a big family; good thing this recipe easily doubles). She made them by spreading softened butter on Royal Lunch Crackers (aka "milk" crackers) and toasting them. Nonnie's brand of milk crackers have (tragically) been discontinued, and when I asked my husband if I could make them with saltines for this book, he said absolutely not. Sadly, for him (but not for you), I did not heed his advice.

1. Heat the oven to 375°F. Line a baking sheet with parchment paper.

2. Place the crackers in a single layer on the prepared baking sheet. Pour the melted butter into a shallow dish and dunk each cracker in the butter, submerging it and then returning it to its place on the pan.

3. Bake for about 10 minutes, or until browned. Serve warm or room temperature, at breakfast, for hordes of kids (or for those that are kids at heart), or at any time that the fried cracker craving hits.

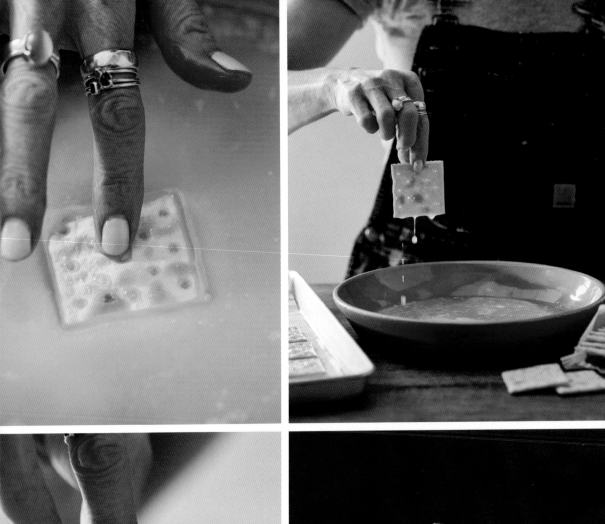

Easy Baked Parmesan Garlic Frico

MAKES 14 FRICO
ACTIVE TIME: 5 MINUTES
BAKE TIME: 7 TO 10 MINUTES

1 cup (100 g) finely
    grated Parmesan
1 teaspoon garlic powder
¼ teaspoon freshly ground
    black pepper

VARIATION

For Easy Baked Parmesan
"Everything" Frico, prepare
the frico as instructed but
omit the garlic powder and
substitute an "everything"
blend of 1¼ teaspoons of
poppy seeds or black sesame
seeds, ½ teaspoon of sesame
seeds, ½ teaspoon of dried
garlic flakes, and ½ teaspoon
of dried minced onion.

Lacy cheese crackers with garlic for the win. These are as easy-peasy as they come—as all you do is melt small mounds of grated cheese on a parchment-lined pan in the oven for 7 minutes and you've got frico-ing (aka freaking) frico. They can be molded into shapes when still warm and are lovely with a glass of wine or crumbled over a salad. Flavor them as you see fit—I'm partial to the combo of garlic and black pepper and the accompanying "everything" variation, but paprika and cayenne might be nice, as would Italian seasoning blend or za'atar. The world is your frico.

1. Heat the oven to 375°F. Line two baking sheets with parchment paper.

2. Whisk together the Parmesan, garlic powder, and pepper in a small bowl. Evenly place 1-tablespoon mounds of the seasoned cheese 1 inch apart on each prepared baking sheet and flatten them gently with your fingers.

3. Bake for 7 to 10 minutes, until the Parm is melted and lightly browned. Remove the frico from the oven and let cool completely before serving.

Zingy Cayenne "Matzos"

MAKES 4 PIECES OF MATZOS
ACTIVE TIME: 10 MINUTES
BAKE TIME: 8 TO 10 MINUTES
PER SHEET

MATZOS
1½ cups (195 g) all-purpose
 flour, plus more for dusting
¾ teaspoon kosher salt
1 teaspoon cayenne pepper,
 or to taste
⅓ cup (77 g) water, at
 room temperature
3 tablespoons neutral oil

PAPRIKA OIL
3 tablespoons neutral oil
½ teaspoon paprika
Flaky sea salt for sprinkling

These matzos are not traditional and certainly not kosher, but they ARE very tasty and very spicy. And did I mention they are also VERY moreish? Because they are. If the dough springs back on itself as you roll it out, as it is wont to do, let it rest a few minutes. And when rolled extra thin, the matzos bake extra fast, so please be mindful. No need to line your baking sheet with parchment when whipping up these zingy "crackers."

1. Heat the oven to 475°F and place a baking sheet inside it.

2. Make the matzos: Whisk together the flour, salt, and cayenne in a large bowl. Pour in the water and oil and stir with a flexible spatula until a shaggy dough forms. Transfer the dough to a lightly floured work surface and knead until smooth. Divide the dough into four pieces (about 78 g each). Thinly roll out each piece with a rolling pin into a rectangle or square, if you are feeling fussy, or a funny oblong shape, if you are channeling me.

3. Make the paprika oil: Whisk together the oil and paprika in a small bowl. Brush the matzo dough shapes with the oil mixture and sprinkle with flaky salt. Re-roll two of the shapes a final time prebake, dock with a fork, remove the hot baking sheet from the oven with pot holder–clad hands and place the docked dough on top.

4. Bake for a total of 8 to 10 minutes (thinner matzos bake faster), carefully flipping the matzos over halfway through the bake time (if you do it quickly, it won't burn your fingers). Remove from the oven and immediately brush with additional paprika oil.

5. Repeat with the remaining two matzos on the same hot baking sheet. Let cool before serving.

CHAPTER 7

All Day I Dream about Snacks

Yes, yes, yes: before you say anything else I did indeed borrow the title of this chapter from Ali Slagle's fantastic cookbook *I Dream of Dinner (so You Don't Have To)*. Snack dreaming is a thing, in case you didn't know, and I am the queen of doing so. Thus, this chapter is chock-full of snacky items that make for delicious party nibbles. They're easy to make (duh); they're tinier than some of the other salty, cheesy, herby, crispy goodies herein; and they are extremely shareable. Many of them cry out to be poured into a large bowl for easy handful-grabbing; others deserve a platter or even a tall glass—Pepper Jack Cheese Straws (page 214), I'm looking at you—of their own. I mean, everyone who parties loves warm, fluffy cheese buns—here, you'll find both traditional gougères (page 202) and gluten-free *pão de queijo* (page 204). And you know what else party-goers love? Party Mix (particularly when miso and garlic are in attendance, page 209), Brie wrapped in puff pastry (page 198), and Baked Mac-n-Cheese Bites (page 201)—in short, folks, nothing brings the revelers to the celebration like savory snacks.

Pro Tips, Fun Facts, and Storing/Reheating Instructions:

- When making Eve's "Cheesy" Buttery Popcorn (page 210), **don't be afraid to vigorously shake your pot when you are trying to coat your corn in butter and "cheese."** Gentle shaking doesn't cut it when complete coverage is the goal.

- The **Pepper Jack Cheese Straws (page 214) can be a little tricky to assemble**, as you need to cut such thin strips of dough. However, the dough is so forgiving that if one of your straws rips when you move it to the baking sheet, just pinch it back together with your fingers.

- Fun fact: The **Roasted Chili Lime Almonds (page 213)** were the fan favorite at the book's photoshoot. Go figure.

TO STORE/REHEAT: Snacks are an inherently unique (and beloved) category of snackable bakes and as such, storage/reheating instructions have been incorporated into each recipe.

Puff Pastry Baked Brie with Favorite Jam

MAKES ONE WHEEL BAKED BRIE

ACTIVE TIME: 5 MINUTES

BAKE TIME: 30 TO 35 MINUTES

One 8.6-ounce (244 g) sheet store-bought frozen puff pastry, thawed

One 8-ounce (227 g) wheel Brie, about 5 inches in diameter

2 tablespoons of your favorite jam, plus more for serving

The Ultimate Egg Wash (page 230)

VARIATION

For Puff Pastry Baked Brie with Caramelized Onions, replace the jam with 3 tablespoons of Quick (Yet Tastiest) Caramelized Onions (page 237).

Melted, runny cheese is up there with one of life's greatest pleasures and one of my favorite food groups. And baked Brie is nothing if not a celebration of melty cheese at its finest. I love it with jam—for the sweet and salty vibes. And, of course, when you wrap it in puff pastry, you're halfway to ambrosia every time. Check out the onion variation that turns this Brie into more of a dinner sitch. A pro tip that might seem obvious: if using a smaller Brie, cut your circle of puff smaller; a larger Brie, cut a larger circle.

──────────

1. Heat the oven to 400°F. Have ready a baking sheet.

2. Place the puff pastry, flour side down, on a sheet of parchment and roll it out until it is about ⅛ inch thick (about an 11-inch square). Set the wheel of Brie in the center of the pastry square and trim the pastry into a circle so there is a 3-inch(ish) bare border around the cheese—really, you just want to make sure there is enough puff to fold up and over the Brie to fully encase it. Spread the jam over the Brie to cover.

3. Fold the puff pastry up and over the jam-topped cheese, stretching it a bit to reach the center, brushing it with egg wash as you do so—this will help one fold of pastry adhere to another as you pleat it. Use your fingers to tighten up, smooth and round out the pastry. Brush the entire pastry-wrapped Brie with egg wash. The puff pastry must be cool when you place it in the oven, so if it warms up once wrapped around the Brie, place the entire shebang in the refrigerator for about 10 minutes before baking.

4. Bake for 30 to 35 minutes, until puffed and browned. Don't worry if the pastry opens up galette style while it bakes—I think it's awfully pretty that way. Remove from the oven and let rest for 20 to 30 minutes to avoid the molten lava that is freshly baked Brie . . . or don't. Serve with extra jam and spoons, so each of your guests can dig in (joke—not really). If you see a little clear liquid seep out the bottom of the Brie when you first cut into it, simply wipe it off your serving platter. It's no biggie.

5. Baked Brie is best served fresh from the oven and still warm, but will last, in an airtight container, in the refrigerator for 3 days. To reheat, bring to room temperature, wrap in foil, and place in a 300°F oven until warm, about 10 minutes.

Baked Mac-n-Cheese Bites

MAKES 24 BITES
ACTIVE TIME: 15 MINUTES
BAKE TIME: ABOUT 10 MINUTES

½ pound (227 g) small
   elbow macaroni

1 teaspoon kosher salt

¾ cup (180 g) whole milk

2 large eggs

¼ cup (56 g) unsalted butter,
   melted and cooled slightly

½ teaspoon freshly ground
   black pepper

¼ teaspoon cayenne pepper

½ teaspoon mustard powder

¾ teaspoon garlic powder

2¾ cups (275 g) shredded
   extra-sharp orange
   Cheddar, plus more
   for sprinkling

One of my all-time fave mac-n-cheese recipes is Millie Peartree's from the *New York Times*. I was lucky enough to interview the lovely Millie for my baking podcast, *She's My Cherry Pie*, and made sure to tell her as much. Her recipe calls for copious amounts of cheese and eggs, and when developing these bites, I leaned into Millie's recipe (i.e., lots of cheese and eggs are both on my ingredient list). Orange cheese gives me all the nostalgic Kraft brand mac-n-cheese feels, but if you're after a different set of feels, don't let me stand in the way. You can make larger bites (chomps?) in a regular 12-well muffin tin.

1. Heat the oven to 425°F. Grease a 24-well mini muffin tin with cooking spray.

2. Cook the macaroni in a large pot of salted, boiling water on the stovetop until al dente, about 5 minutes. Drain the pasta and set aside. Give the pot a quick rinse in cold water to cool it, and whisk in the milk, eggs, melted butter, salt, black pepper, cayenne, and mustard and garlic powders. Stir in the hot pasta, and then the cheese with a flexible spatula to combine. Place the pot over medium to medium-high heat and stir for about 5 minutes, or until the cheese melts and the sauce thickens.

3. Place 2-tablespoon portions of mac-n-cheese in each muffin tin well and sprinkle each bite with a bit more shredded Cheddar. Bake for about 10 minutes, or until lightly browned and melty. Remove from the oven and let sit for 5 minutes before removing the bites from the tin and serving.

4. The bites are best served fresh from the oven and still warm, but will last, in an airtight container, in the refrigerator for 3 days or in the freezer for up to a month. Reheat room temperature ones on a parchment-lined baking sheet in a 300°F oven until warm, 5 to 10 minutes.

Straight-Up Gruyère Gougères

MAKES ABOUT 30 GOUGÈRES
ACTIVE TIME: 15 MINUTES
BAKE TIME: 20 TO 22 MINUTES

½ cup (113 g) unsalted butter

1 cup (240 g) nonfat milk or water, or ½ cup whole milk plus ½ cup water

½ teaspoon kosher salt

½ teaspoon freshly ground black pepper

1 cup (130 g) all-purpose flour

4 large eggs, at room temperature

1½ cups (150 g) shredded Gruyère

Gougères are light and airy cheese puffs that can be assembled in minutes with no special equipment needed. Yes, folks do make them using a food processor or stand mixer, but we easy-peasy bakers do not. You can make smaller gougères with a 1-tablespoon portion scoop or measuring spoon, and if you do so, you'll be the proud parent of 48 mini puffs. Congrats to you and the kids.

1. Heat the oven to 400°F. Line two baking sheets with parchment paper.

2. Combine the butter, milk, salt, and pepper in a medium saucepan and bring to a boil over medium-high heat. Lower the heat to medium, add the flour, and stir until combined with a wooden spoon or flexible spatula. Continue to cook the dough until it's smooth, thick, comes together in a mass, and a film begins to form on the bottom of the pan, about 2 minutes. Transfer the dough to a large heatproof bowl and vigorously stir for about 1 minute, until cooled a bit. Add the eggs, one at a time, beating vigorously after each until fully incorporated. Stir in the cheese.

3. Portion the dough using a 1½-tablespoon portion scoop, if you have one, or two spoons—each will be about the size of a golf ball—onto the prepared sheets, leaving about 2 inches between them.

4. Bake for 20 to 22 minutes, rotating the sheets at the halfway point and swapping their placement in the oven, until the gougères are lightly browned and puffy. Repeat with any remaining dough. Serve warm.

5. Gougères are best served fresh from the oven and still warm, but will last, in an airtight container, in the refrigerator for 3 days or in the freezer for up to a month. Reheat room-temperature gougères on a parchment-lined baking sheet in a 300°F oven until warm, about 5 minutes.

Gluten-Free Cheese Buns (aka Pão de Queijo)

MAKES 28 PUFFS
ACTIVE TIME: 15 MINUTES
REST TIME: 10 MINUTES
BAKE TIME: ABOUT 20 MINUTES

1 cup (240 g) nonfat or 2% milk, or ½ cup whole milk plus ½ cup water

½ cup (113 g) unsalted butter, or neutral oil

1 teaspoon kosher salt

2 cups (260 g) tapioca flour/ starch

2 large eggs

¾ cup (75 g) finely grated Pecorino Romano or Parmesan

1 cup (100 g) shredded low-moisture whole-milk mozzarella

These are not exactly *quintessential* pao de queijo (aka Brazilian cheese bread/buns) due to their more craggy exterior, and chewy, slightly dense interior. But they are still wildly delicious in that must-eat-many kind of way. Poke the bottom of each bun with the handle of a wooden spoon pre-bake, leaving an indentation, for buns that bake more evenly (thanks, *Serious Eats* and Sohla El-Waylly, for the tip).

1. Heat the oven to 400°F. Line two baking sheets with parchment paper.

2. Combine the milk, butter, and salt in a medium saucepan and bring to a boil over medium-high heat. Remove from the heat, add the tapioca flour, and stir until incorporated, using a wooden spoon. Transfer the dough to a large, heatproof bowl and stir vigorously for about 1 minute, and then let rest about 10 minutes until no longer hot to the touch, stirring occasionally. Add the eggs, one at a time, stirring vigorously after each until combined. Add the two cheeses and knead the mixture in the bowl with your hands for about 2 minutes, or until fully incorporated.

3. Portion the dough using a 1½-tablespoon portion scoop, if you have one, or two spoons (about 30 g, or the size of a golf ball) equally between the prepared pans. Roll each ball in your hands to smooth out the exterior. Then, cupping each one in your hand, poke a ½-inch indentation in the ball's bottom with the handle of a wooden spoon.

4. Bake for about 20 minutes, rotating the sheets at the halfway point and swapping their placement in the oven, until the buns are lightly browned and puffy. Serve warm.

5. The buns are best served fresh from the oven, still warm and stretchy, but will last in an airtight container overnight or frozen for up to a month. Reheat room-temp buns on a parchment-lined baking sheet in a 300°F oven until warm, 5 to 10 minutes.

Kristin's Olive and Cheese Puffs

MAKES ABOUT 35 TINY PUFFS
ACTIVE TIME: 10 MINUTES
REST TIME: 45 MINUTES
BAKE TIME: 20 TO 25 MINUTES

¼ cup (56 g) unsalted butter,
    melted and cooled slightly
½ teaspoon paprika
¼ teaspoon cayenne pepper
¼ teaspoon kosher salt
1 cup (100 g) shredded
    Monterey Jack, or your
    fave cheese
½ cup (65 g) all-purpose flour
About 35 small pimiento-
    stuffed olives, half(ish)
    of a 7-ounce jar,
    drained and dried

VARIATION

For Cheese Puff Cookies, omit the olives and roll the dough into 2-teaspoon (14 g) balls and evenly space them on a parchment-lined baking sheet. Freeze for about 45 minutes and then bake at 350°F for about 15 minutes, or until lightly browned. Makes about 15 tiny cookies.

My SIL, Kristin, is an entertaining queen with many fun and festive recipes in her fab repertoire, including these joyful little retro cheesy-wrapped olives. The combo of the paprika-flavored dough and the briny olives is just what every-party-you-are-ever-going-to-throw asked for. Some of Kristin's tips for perfect puffs, include purchasing the smallest Manzanilla olives you can find and drying them as best you can on a paper towel–lined plate before wrapping them in the dough. She also makes and freezes these cutest of puffs for all the fantastic parties her future self will be throwing. Be warned: a resting time is required for perfect puffs but it's worth it, I promise.

1. Line a baking sheet with parchment paper.

2. Whisk together the melted butter, paprika, cayenne, and salt in a medium bowl. Fold in the cheese and flour with a flexible spatula. Wrap a teaspoon of dough around each olive, rolling it in your hands to cover, then placing the wrapped olives on the prepared baking sheet. Place the sheet in the freezer for about 45 minutes. Heat the oven to 350°F.

3. Bake for 20 to 25 minutes, rotating at the halfway point, until dry and lightly browned. Serve immediately.

4. Olive puffs are best served fresh from the oven and still warm, but will last, in an airtight container, in the refrigerator for 3 days or in the freezer for up to a month. Reheat them directly from the refrigerator or freezer on a parchment-lined baking sheet in a 300°F oven until warm, about 10 to 15 minutes, depending on whether they are cold or frozen.

Miso Garlic Butter Party Mix

MAKES ABOUT 12 CUPS
ACTIVE TIME: 5 MINUTES
BAKE TIME: 45 MINUTES

4 cups (125 g) Corn Chex or
   similar cereal
4 cups (125 g) Rice Chex or
   similar cereal
1 cup (100 g) pecans,
   coarsely chopped
1 sleeve (105 g) butter crackers,
   such as Ritz, about
   32 crackers
1½ cups (45 g) Bugles or similar
   corn snack
2 teaspoons garlic powder
10 tablespoons (141 g) unsalted
   butter, melted and warm
5 tablespoons (82 g) white
   miso, at room temperature
1½ teaspoons kosher salt
¾ teaspoon freshly ground
   black pepper

Chex Mix is a mind-bogglingly tasty snack, particularly when you add Bugles and Ritz crackers to the mix and reach for Chex of the corn and rice varieties, exclusively. Or is that just me? If you prefer pretzels to Bugles, wheat Chex to rice/corn, and saltines or another cracker to Ritz, by all means use them. Pro tip: If you are pro-Ritz, but the size bums you out when you're grabbing a handful and can't easily shove all of it down your gullet, feel free to break those babies up, or use Mini Ritz.

1. Heat the oven to 250°F. Line two baking sheets with parchment paper.

2. Toss together the cereals, pecans, crackers, and Bugles in a large bowl with your hands or a flexible spatula. Whisk the garlic powder into the melted butter in a small bowl and then vigorously whisk in the miso until emulsified—the mixture might look broken at first, but it will come together with a little elbow grease. Whisk in the salt and pepper. Pour half of the miso butter over the cereal mixture and toss to coat (hands are the best tool for this, FYI). Pour in the remaining miso butter and toss a final time.

3. Divide equally between the prepared baking sheets, spreading the mixture into an even layer, and bake for about 45 minutes, stirring every 15 minutes and swapping the placement of the sheets in the oven at the 30-minute mark. Remove from the oven and let cool to room temperature before serving.

4. Party Mix will last, in an airtight container, on the counter for about a week.

Eve's "Cheesy" Buttery Popcorn

MAKES ABOUT 10 CUPS
ACTIVE TIME: 5 MINUTES

10 cups (100 g) popped
    popcorn, unsalted (from
    ½ cup prepopped kernels)
½ cup (113 g) unsalted butter,
    melted, or olive oil
⅓ cup (22 g) nutritional yeast
1¼ teaspoons kosher salt

I adore popcorn. Like, it's one of my favorite foods, hands down, and although I consider myself a bit of a popcorn connoisseur, I had never had it with nutritional yeast until my younger son, Jack, whipped up a batch in my kitchen for some kids he was babysitting. He apparently learned about it from Eve (his charges' mom) and I went absolutely bananas for it; as the nutritional yeast adds the most delicious of cheesy, buttery, and nutty flavors to the corn. I, of course, am quite butter-forward and so, yes this recipe calls for an entire stick—but you can use less—such as 6 tablespoons for instance—or even olive oil. Evenly coating the corn with the butter, yeast, and salt is a bit of an art form, which you will be happy to hear that I have mastered and shared herein.

1. Place the popcorn in a large pot with a lid—if you just used one to pop the corn, use it (and goody for you). Transfer the melted butter to a liquid measuring cup and pour one-third to half of the butter over the popcorn. Place the lid on the pot and shake it vigorously. Repeat once or twice more with the remaining butter until all of it coats the popcorn.

2. Sprinkle the nutritional yeast and salt over the popcorn and repeat the vigorous lidded-pot shaking until all of the popcorn is coated. If some of the yeast sticks to the bottom of the pot, use a flexible spatula or your hands to dislodge it in between shakes. Serve immediately.

3. Popcorn is best served right after its been coated, but will last, in an airtight container, on the counter overnight. Refresh it, if desired, on a parchment-lined baking sheet in a 250°F oven until warm, about 5 minutes.

Roasted Chili Lime Almonds

MAKES ABOUT 3 CUPS
ACTIVE TIME: 10 MINUTES
BAKE TIME: 45 MINUTES

3 tablespoons lime zest,
    divided (from 3 to 5 limes
    depending on size)
1 tablespoon kosher salt
1 tablespoon chili powder,
    divided
A rounded ¼ teaspoon
    cayenne pepper
2 tablespoons packed light
    brown sugar
1 large egg white
2 tablespoons freshly
    squeezed lime juice,
    divided (from 1 to 2 limes)
2½ cups (375 g) raw whole
    almonds
Flaky sea salt for sprinkling

A savory snacky baking book deserves a cocktail nut recipe, and here she is. The chili lime salt is just exactly what the nuts in my life have been asking for; I just wasn't listening—until now. An egg white is on the ingredient list, as it really is the best way to get toppings to adhere to nuts. And when the topping includes lime zest and juice, chili, cayenne, and salt? I mean, you *really* don't want to miss out on even a single drop, sprinkle, flake, etc. and you can use the yolk to make the Ultimate Egg Wash (page 230).

1. Heat the oven to 300°F. Line a baking sheet with parchment paper.

2. Rub 2 tablespoons of the zest into the salt with your fingers in a medium bowl. Rub in 2 teaspoons of the chili powder and the cayenne and brown sugar. Whisk together the egg white and 1 tablespoon of the lime juice until frothy in *another* medium bowl. Add the almonds to the egg white mixture and stir with a flexible spatula until well coated. Transfer the wet nuts into the bowl of sweetened chili lime salt and toss to combine.

3. Evenly spread the nuts onto the prepared baking sheet and bake for 45 minutes, stirring every 15 minutes. (The easiest way to stir is to remove the baking sheet from the oven, place it on the counter, carefully grab hold of the corner edge of the paper, and nudge the nuts—which will be stuck to the paper—with a spatula to release them. Then carefully toss the nuts with your hands.) At the 40-minute mark, remove the nuts from the oven and sprinkle the remaining tablespoon of juice and teaspoon of chili powder over the nuts, releasing any stuck ones and carefully tossing to coat with your hands, as you did before. Return the pan to the oven and bake for 5 more minutes. Remove from the oven, sprinkle with flaky salt, and once cooled to room temperature, sprinkle with the remaining zest and serve.

4. The roasted almonds will keep, in an airtight container, on the counter for up to 2 weeks (and maybe longer).

Pepper Jack Cheese Straws

MAKES ABOUT 60 STRAWS
ACTIVE TIME: 15 MINUTES
BAKE TIME: 10 TO 12 MINUTES
PER SHEET

1 cup (130 g) all-purpose flour,
  plus more for dusting
1⅓ cups (133 g) shredded
  pepper Jack cheese, or
  your fave, plus ¼ teaspoon
  cayenne powder for kick
¾ teaspoon kosher salt
¾ cups (180 g) heavy
  cream, cold

So, I basically used my Best-Ever Cream Biscuit Dough (page 234, but sans leavening) to make these statuesque and elegant cheese straws, as recipes for both straws and biscuits call for the same ingredients. Pro tips: If you rest the dough after forming it into a rectangle, it's easier to work with; the baked straws are delicate—as grace and sophistication come at a cost—and as the straws bake, the cheese bubbles out a bit—don't be alarmed.

1. Heat the oven to 400°F. Line two baking sheets with parchment paper.

2. Stir together the flour, cheese, and salt in a large bowl, using a fork. Pour in the cream and stir with a flexible spatula until no loose flour remains. Dump the dough onto a floured work surface. With floured hands, pat the dough into a rectangle. Using a rolling pin, roll the dough into a 12-by-17-inch rectangle, between ⅛ and ¼ inch thick, with a long side facing you. Reflour your work surface and move the dough around as you roll to keep it from sticking.

3. Trim the rectangle to about 10½ by 15 inches. Using a pizza cutter or paring knife, thinly slice the dough lengthwise into ¼-inch-wide strips. Reroll and slice the scraps. Place 16 to 18 strips on each prepared baking sheet, leaving ½ inch between each one—if they tear, press them back together.

4. Bake for 10 to 12 minutes, rotating the sheets at the halfway point and swapping their placement in the oven, until the sticks are lightly browned. Repeat with remaining strips. Let cool and serve.

5. Cheese straws will last, in an airtight container, on the counter for up to 5 days.

Devils on Horseback
WITH CHIVE CREAM CHEESE

MAKES 24 DEVILS
ACTIVE TIME: 10 MINUTES
BAKE TIME: 20 TO 25 MINUTES

6 ounces (170 g) full-fat
cream cheese, at
room temperature

3 tablespoons finely
chopped fresh chives, or
1½ tablespoons dried

¾ teaspoon garlic powder

¼ teaspoon onion powder

½ teaspoon kosher salt

24 large dates, such as
Medjool (about 12 ounces
[340 g]), pitted

12 slices raw thin bacon
(not thick-cut), sliced in
half crosswise

VARIATION

For Devils on Horseback with
Blue Cheese, replace the seasoned cream cheese mixture
with 6 ounces (170 g) of your
fave blue cheese, stuffing
each date with about 1½ teaspoons before wrapping with
bacon.

A "devil on horseback" is traditionally a date stuffed with blue cheese, wrapped in bacon and baked. The sweet date caramelizes, the cheese gets melty and soft, and the bacon does its fatty, salty, crispy thing; and the whole package is just heaven on a toothpick. Here, inspired by my friend Anna Painter's *Food & Wine* recipe for bacon-wrapped dates, I have nixed the blue cheese for chive cream cheese (and, yes, thank you: this was indeed a stroke of genius). The recipe works with turkey bacon, too, if you're a chicken and turkey eater, but pass when it comes to beef and pork—you just might want to drizzle a little olive oil over the dates prebake, as the turkey bacon is less fatty than the piggy stuff. A sprinkling of chopped chives before serving is a hostess-with-the-mostest kind of touch.

1. Heat the oven to 400°F. Line a baking sheet with parchment paper and have ready 24 toothpicks.

2. Combine the cream cheese, chives, garlic and onion powders, and salt in a small bowl, using a fork. Make a slit in each date with a paring knife and stretch it open a bit without tearing it in two. You can even press the date flesh a little to make more space on either side of the slit. Stuff each date with about 1½ teaspoons of cream cheese. Close the slit as best you can (if a little cream cheese pokes out, no worries) and wrap each date with a slice of bacon. Pierce with a toothpick through the middle to secure the bacon and place on the prepared pan.

3. Bake for 20 to 25 minutes, flipping the devils over at the halfway point, so both sides of the bacon get crispy. Serve warm.

4. Devils are best served fresh from the oven and still warm, but will last, in an airtight container, in the refrigerator for 3 days. Reheat room temperature ones on a parchment-lined baking sheet in a 350°F oven until warm, 5 to 10 minutes.

Dad's Pigs in a Blanket

MAKES 48 PIGS
ACTIVE TIME: 15 MINUTES
REST TIME: 20 MINUTES
BAKE TIME: 15 TO 20 MINUTES

All-purpose flour for dusting
One batch Best-Ever Cream
    Biscuit Dough (page 234)
Mayonnaise for brushing
8 (376 g) hot dogs
The Ultimate Egg Wash
    (page 230)

These are for my dad, who adored pigs in a blanket, and who passed away while I was writing this book. He would have loved my easy-peasy version of these dogs, made from my cream biscuit dough, because they are so darn tasty (and because he was one of those dads who kinds-sorta loved everything his daughter made, did, etc.). I think my dad would have dipped his blanketed dogs in mustard, and since I'm fond of the adage "like father, like daughter," I def will be following suit.

━━━━━━━

1. Heat the oven to 425°F. Line two baking sheets with parchment paper.

2. Dump the biscuit dough onto a floured work surface and knead to bring together. Pat the dough into a rectangle. Using a rolling pin, roll the dough into a 5-by-16-inch rectangle with a long side facing you. Brush the dough with the mayo and cut it lengthwise into 8 pieces, 5 by 2 inches each.

3. Place a hot dog on each piece. Wrap the dogs with the dough and pull and pinch to seal. Roll the wrapped dogs on the counter and freeze on one of the prepared sheets for 20 minutes.

4. Slice each wrapped dog into six pieces, trimming excess dough from the ends if necessary. Rotate the wrapped dogs with each cut, to avoid flattening the dough on one side. Equally divide the pieces, hot dog side up, between the two prepared baking sheets. Brush the sides and tops of the "blankets" with egg wash. Freeze for 10 minutes.

5. Bake for 15 to 20 minutes, until lightly browned. Let rest for 10 minutes and serve.

6. Blanketed pigs are best served fresh from the oven but will last, in an airtight container, in the fridge for 3 days, or frozen for up to a month.

Best-Ever Cheesy Sausage Balls

MAKES 20 SAUSAGE BALLS
ACTIVE TIME: 10 MINUTES
BAKE TIME: 15 TO 20 MINUTES

1 cup (130 g) all-purpose flour
1½ teaspoons baking powder
½ teaspoon kosher salt
¼ teaspoon cayenne pepper
2¼ cups (225 g) shredded cheese, your fave, at room temperature
½ pound (227 g) raw bulk pork sausage or links, such as sweet Italian, at room temperature
¼ cup (60 g) whole milk, at room temperature

Oh, gosh—not sure how I grew up in a home without a sausage ball in sight; but I did and I am making up for it now. Traditionally made with Bisquick, these homemade meaty, soft, cheesy balls are easily and enthusiastically consumed one after the other, so be ready, at both breakfast time or as a cocktail snack. Pro tip: Using room-temperature ingredients will make easy work of combining the meat and cheese into the dry ingredients.

1. Heat the oven to 350°F and line a baking sheet with parchment paper.

2. Whisk together the flour, baking powder, salt, and cayenne in a large bowl. Whisk in the cheese and then gently mix in the sausage (removed from the casings if using links) and milk with your hands, or a flexible spatula if you're squeamish—do not overmix, you just want to evenly incorporate all the ingredients. Form the mixture into 1½-tablespoon balls (about 30 g each or the size of a golf ball) with a portion scoop, if you have one, or measuring spoons.

3. Place the balls on the prepared baking sheet and bake for 15 to 20 minutes, rotating at the halfway point, until nicely browned. Serve warm.

4. Sausage balls are best served fresh from the oven and still warm but will last, in an airtight container, in the refrigerator for 3 days, or in the freezer for up to a month. Reheat room temperature ones on a parchment-lined baking sheet in a 300°F oven until warm, 5 to 10 minutes.

Dolly's Melty Cheese Squares

WITH CHILI CRISP

Dolly is Kathy's mom, and Kathy is my Milwaukee pen pal, an epic home baker, a generous sharer of recipes, and a grandmother, to boot. Apparently, as a girl, Kathy used to make these squares whenever her parents were entertaining, for their cocktail party or dinner guests. And, no, she did not add chili crisp oil to them in the early 1960s—that is all me, in the 2020s. If Velveeta gives you pause, I apologize, but it is, hands down, the perfect melty cheese in which to dunk toast squares, and any leftover sauce can be heated up and drizzled on tortilla chips (nachos, anyone?).

MAKES 32 SQUARES

ACTIVE TIME: 10 MINUTES

BROIL TIME: 1 TO 2 MINUTES PER SHEET

8 slices white square sandwich bread, such as Pepperidge Farm brand

½ pound (227 g) Velveeta, or your fave melty-forward cheese

½ cup (120 g) heavy cream

½ cup (113 g) unsalted butter

2 teaspoons chili crisp oil, or more to taste, plus more oil plus crisp for garnish

1. Adjust an oven rack so it is about 6 inches below your broiler and turn on the broiler. Line two baking sheets with aluminum foil and place them near your stovetop.

2. Place the slices of bread in a single layer on one of the prepared baking sheets. Toast the bread under the broiler, 30 to 60 seconds per side, watching closely so they don't burn. Remove from the broiler and cut each slice of toast into four equal squares. Leave the broiler on.

3. Heat the cheese, cream, and butter together in a saucepan on the stovetop over medium to medium-high heat until the cheese and butter melt, stirring frequently with a flexible spatula. Once melted, add the chili crisp oil and stir to combine.

4. Lower the heat to low and dunk one side of each toast square in the warm cheese sauce, letting the excess drip off. Evenly divide the pieces of toast, cheese side up, between the two prepared baking sheets. Broil, one sheet at a time, for 30 to 45 seconds, until the topping is bubbly and has a few dark brown spots. Using a small spoon, drizzle the toast squares with additional oil and chili crisp and serve immediately. Dolly's squares are not great on day two, so get 'em while they're hot.

Some Snacky Board Suggestions

I hope it goes without saying that you may combine any and EVERY small bite, treat, hand pie, dish, or baked good in this book with any other (or with many others), and call it a meal, a snack, a board, or a good time. Here, I've created a few different extremely harmonious snackable collections for different moments of the day—from sunup to sundown—just for inspo in case you love absolutely EVERYTHING in every chapter (I mean, of course you do) and just can't bear to choose.

The Brunch'y Snack Board
Brekkie never had it this good.
- Jenny's Egg Puffs with Prosciutto Bottoms (page 84)
- Eggy Cheesy Open-Face Tarts (page 117)
- Best-Ever Cheesy Sausage Balls (page 221)
- Everything Bagel and Cream Cheese Snacking "Bread" (page 68)
- Nonnie's Crackers in the Oven (page 188)

The "Girl Lunch" Snack Board
Yes, you're right: this board has a cheese theme, as girl lunch demands it.
- Grilled Cheese Sandwich Tart (page 95)
- Butter Crackers with Melty Cheese and Sour Pickles (page 187)
- Devils on Horseback with Chive Cream Cheese (page 217)
- Kristin's Olive and Cheese Puffs (page 207)
- Eve's "Cheesy" Buttery Popcorn (page 210)

The Cocktail Snack Board
Tasty treats to accompany any and all the drinks.
- Cocktail Hour Loaf (page 64)
- Dad's Pigs in a Blanket (page 218)
- Miso Garlic Butter Party Mix (page 209)
- Fire Crackers (page 184)
- Easy Baked Parmesan Garlic Frico (page 191)

The Date "Dinner" Snack Board
Delicious delicacies for dates with others or yourself.
- Baked Mac-n-Cheese Bites (page 201)
- Pom's Boxing Day Sausage Rolls (page 92)
- Zucchini Parm Scarpaccia (page 145)
- Cream Cheese and Olive Pinwheels (page 172)
- Dolly's Melty Cheese Squares with Chili Crisp (page 222)

CHAPTER 8

The Essential Savory Hacks

When I savory cook—okay, when I enter the kitchen, period—I am always on the lookout for a hack, a shortcut, an easy-peasy trick. When I decided to write this cookbook, I knew we would need plenty of hacks, so that the recipes were as easy-peasy as I wanted them/needed them to be. The six in this chapter feature prominently in many of the salty, cheesy, herby, crispy snackable bakes herein, and are worth turning to, well, constantly, even when you're not snackable baking—though that probably never happens, right?

Pro Tips, Fun Facts, and Storing/Reheating Instructions:

- **Everyone makes egg wash a little differently**, and although I think my way is the best way, if you love mixing your egg with a splash of water or milk or cream—or don't like adding anything—be my guest.

- I've been known to eat a bowl of well-seasoned **4-Minute Mushrooms** (page 238), maybe with a sprinkling of Parm, for dinner, as mushrooms are my everything.

- **Bacon takes a while to render its fat and get supercrispy**, even Fast and Dirty (Not Literally) Bacon (page 241). But freezing and then cutting the bacon into ½-inch pieces before cooking, truly makes a world of difference.

TO STORE/REHEAT: Each of these hacks is so different from the other that the storage/reheating instructions have been incorporated into each recipe.

The Ultimate Egg Wash

1 large egg, at room temperature (if you remember to bring your egg to room temp, it will blend more easily, but if you do not, no biggie)

⅛ teaspoon kosher salt

Everyone has a different way of making an egg wash, and this is mine. I learned the trick of whisking salt with the egg—rather than water or milk, as is more traditional—from my pal Zoë Kanan. She explained that salt is a great addition to a wash, as it breaks down the white, making it much easier to brush (you're welcome). And, no, you're right: I don't usually make egg wash in such enormous quantities as is pictured here, but makes for a good photo, no?

———

1. Whisk the egg and salt together in a small bowl, using a fork, until the white and yolk are thoroughly blended.

2. The Ultimate Egg Wash will last, tightly wrapped, in the refrigerator for 3 to 5 days.

Magic Melted Butter Pie Dough

Melted butter pie dough is quite literally my everything. It is a breeze to assemble as there is no resting and no chilling and no nothing. Moreover, it is delicious and buttery, more crisp than flaky, superflavorful, and such a dream to work with that you may never go back to the world of cold butter again. It is easiest to work with when it is first assembled and still warm from the hot milk and butter.

× 1
2 cups (260 g) all-purpose flour
¾ teaspoon kosher salt
1 teaspoon granulated sugar
½ teaspoon baking powder
½ cup (113 g) unsalted butter, cubed
¼ cup (60 g) whole milk

× 1½
3 cups (390 g) all-purpose flour
1 rounded teaspoon kosher salt
1½ teaspoons granulated sugar
¾ teaspoon baking powder
¾ cup (170 g) unsalted butter, cubed
¼ cup plus 2 tablespoons (90 g) whole milk

SINGLE CRUST
1¾ cups (228 g) all-purpose flour
½ teaspoon kosher salt
¾ teaspoon granulated sugar
½ teaspoon baking powder
½ cup (113 g) unsalted butter, cubed
3 tablespoons whole milk

1. To make your dough of choice, whisk together the flour, salt, sugar, and baking powder (and the cheese or basil, if your recipe calls for it) in a large bowl.

2. Heat the butter and milk in either a 2-cup glass measuring cup, if you have one, or a glass bowl in a microwave on HIGH, in three 30-second bursts, stirring in between each, or in a small saucepan on the stovetop over medium-high heat, until the butter is melted and the milk is steaming hot—the mixture doesn't need to boil.

3. Pour the hot liquid over the flour mixture and stir with a fork until the mixture holds together when squeezed.

4. If you are preparing the dough for a single crust pie, transfer it to your pie plate. If you are preparing the dough for hand pies, galettes, or mini pies, turn out the dough onto a work surface and knead a few times until smooth. In either case, use immediately.

VARIATIONS

× 1 WITH PARMESAN: ½ cup (50 g) finely grated Parmesan
× 1 WITH BASIL: 1 teaspoon dried basil

Best-Ever Cream Biscuit Dough

1 cup (130 g) all-purpose flour

1 cup (120 g) cake flour

1½ tablespoons granulated sugar

1 tablespoon plus 1 teaspoon baking powder

1 teaspoon kosher salt

1½ cups (360 g) heavy cream

I don't know what to tell you: this biscuit dough is the stuff of legends and not only makes fantastically light and tender biscuits, but can also be transformed into so many other wonderful baked goods. She's basically unstoppable. Now, I do like a mixture of all-purpose and cake flour here, for a dough that bakes up ultratender, but if that seems fussy to you, then just use 2 cups of all-purpose *or* turn to page 20 to check out my hack for making your own cake flour.

———

1. Whisk together the flours, sugar, baking powder, and salt (and cheese, if your recipe calls for it) in a large bowl. Add the cream and stir with a flexible spatula until no loose flour remains. Use immediately.

VARIATION

WITH PARMESAN: ¾ cup (75 g) finely grated Parmesan

Quickest (Yet Tastiest) Caramelized Onions

Who doesn't love caramelized onions? But—and more importantly—who actually hates how long they take to cook? Uhm, me. I am not a fan—I'm too impatient and I'd just rather skip a recipe that calls for them than make them. But no longer! These onions here are pure magic AND they take only 15 minutes. Amazing, I know.

MAKES ABOUT 1 CUP (240 G)

1 tablespoon olive oil, plus
    more if needed
1 pound yellow onions,
    sliced thinly
⅛ teaspoon baking soda
½ teaspoon kosher salt
1 tablespoon balsamic vinegar

1. Heat a Dutch oven or cast-iron skillet (a dark pan is helpful, but not required) over medium-high to high heat. Once hot, add the olive oil and onion slices. Stir to coat the onions in the oil and let cook for about 7 minutes, stirring every 2 minutes or so, but not continuously. If the pan seems very dry and the onions are sticking a lot, lower the heat and/or add an extra tablespoon of oil.

2. Sprinkle the baking soda and salt over the onions, stir to coat and continue to stir almost constantly for another 8 minutes, scraping the fond from the pan, until nicely browned.

3. Remove from the heat and stir in the vinegar. Bring to room temperature before using (to do so quickly, spread out on a dinner plate and pop in the freezer for a few minutes).

4. Quickest (Yet Tastiest) Caramelized Onions will last, tightly wrapped, in the refrigerator for up to a week.

4-Minute Mushrooms

2 cups (227 g) assorted mushrooms, chopped coarsely

Microwave mushrooms FTW! (Sorry, haters.) I mean, I have absolutely nothing against sautéed mushrooms on the stovetop or roasted mushrooms in the oven, and if you want to make me a big plate, I will love you forever. But I dig a tasty shortcut, and this is one of those.

1. Place the mushrooms in a microwave-safe bowl. Cover and microwave on HIGH for about 4 minutes, stirring periodically, until the mushrooms are collapsed and tender.

2. Drain the mushrooms before seasoning, as they give off water as they cook. Let cool to room temperature before using.

3. 4-Minute Mushrooms will last, tightly wrapped, in the refrigerator for 3 to 5 days.

Fast and Dirty (Not Literally) Bacon

½ pound (226 g) bacon, slightly frozen, cut into ½-inch pieces

I love bacon when someone else makes it for me. But making it myself? Not so much. However, cutting the strips into ½-inch pieces before doing so is a game-changer—I promise. And if the bacon is slightly frozen when you cut it? Game-changer × 100. Yes: it is best to cook bacon low and slow to render the most fat, and yes, as an easy-peasy baker, I take issue with that. But just know that I wouldn't ask you to do it if it wasn't worth it.

1. Place the bacon in a cold skillet over medium-low heat and cook until crispy, about 15 to 20 minutes. Pour off the fat into a small heatproof container, if it will be used for other purposes, such as in Kathy's Old-Fasioned Cracklin' Bread (page 75), and drain the bacon on a paper towel–lined plate.

2. Fast and Dirty (not literally) Bacon will last in an air-tight container in the refrigerator for 3 to 5 days.

Acknowledgments

So many peeps contributed to this book and to my delicious transformation from a lover of baking sweets to a lover of baking with cheese (and other savory ingredients . . .).

My beloved friend and recipe tester extraordinaire, Stephanie Whitten, is a brilliant baker when the ingredients run sweet, but is also an incredibly talented *savory* baker and cook. Steph played an integral role in making every recipe herein tastier than it was when I first shared it with her, and she taught me so much about my spice drawer along the way.

Big thanks, as always, to my wonderful agent, Judy Linden, and to the incredible team at Countryman, whose commitment to spreading the snackable bakes ethos is as steadfast as my own. Thank you to my editor (and friend!), Ann Treistman, for spearheading that commitment, and to Countryman's crazy-talented art director, Allison Chi, who I adore.

Back when savory baking and I were just getting acquainted and this book was in its infancy, the team at Postcard PR—Olga, Hannah, and Liza—helped immeasurably in unpacking with me which recipes made sense to include in a baking book such as this. And I am so grateful to them for that. And to the team at Mona Creative, for getting the word out about just how fab those recipes (and this now grown-up book) ended up being.

Nico Shinco, Kaitlyn Wayne, and Maeve Sheridan are three of my favorite people—and also the dreamiest of photo dream teams. Every day of the two-week photo shoot they made me feel like a supermodel/movie star (which ain't a bad way to feel, I gotta tell you). Loving, supportive, and wildly talented doesn't begin to describe these three people.

Also on set were Caroline Saunders and Claire Fan, both of whom reached out to me cold (Caroline via DM and Claire via email) to see if I might need any help with the book (spoiler alert: the answer was yes). Not only did each of them test countless recipes for me, but they enthusiastically assisted Katie and Steph with photo prep and were each such an absolute pleasure to have around. Look out for those two: I know they will each do great things.

A special thanks to Regan Murray, too, who also contacted me cold via DM and was instrumental in helping me develop my (genius) caramelized onion hack. And to Melinda Stubbee, who tested recipes for the book, helped immeasurably with my newsletters, and credits me with introducing her to the joys of one-bowl baking (thank you very much).

Finally, to my Cherry Bombe family, Kerry Diamond, Catherine Baker, Kate Miller Spencer, et al. So grateful to be a member of the squad—you are all my cherry pies. And to my actual family, Matt, Oliver, and Jack (and Knibbie and Ray Ray, too): my days are all sweeter (and often saltier—in a good way) because of you.

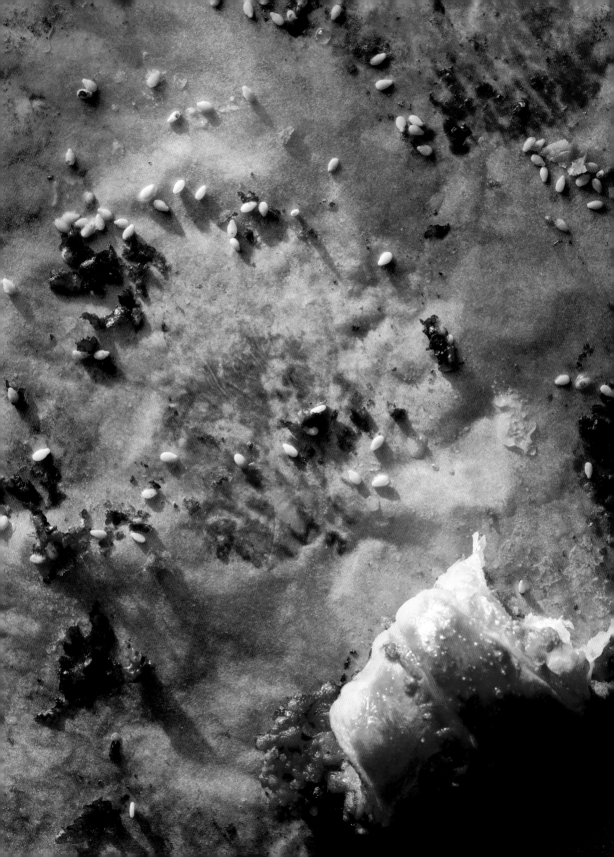

Index

Page numbers in *italics* indicate illustrations.